STO

✓

Critical acclaim for *Cracking the Pacific Rim* . . .

"*Cracking the Pacific Rim* provides a wealth of critical information for entering the booming Pacific markets. It is a much needed and excellent, comprehensive guide for business executives. If there is only one business book that gets packed on your next trip abroad, this definitely should be it."

> *Lew W. Cramer*
> Assistant Vice President-Federal Relations
> US West, Inc.

"Country by country, detail by detail, a truly comprehensive guide to trading with the world's fastest growing markets — a valuable reference for doing business in the global marketplace."

> *Janet Harris-Lange*
> President
> National Association of Women Business Owners

"A goldmine for investors assessing business opportunities in the Pacific Rim. Terrific information for both small/individual investors and larger corporations."

> *Erin Sibley*
> Satellite Communications Analyst
> for a large aerospace firm

CRACKING THE PACIFIC RIM

EVERYTHING

MARKETERS

MUST KNOW

TO SELL

INTO THE

WORLD'S

NEWEST

EMERGING

MARKETS

**ENDERLYN
DZIGGEL**

PROBUS PUBLISHING COMPANY
Chicago, Illinois
Cambridge, England

© 1992, Allyn Enderlyn and Oliver C. Dziggel

This publication is designed to provide accurate and authoritative information in regard to the subject matter covered. It is sold with the understanding that the publisher is not engaged in rendering legal, accounting or other professional service.

ISBN 1-55738-254-9

Printed in the United States of America

EB

1 2 3 4 5 6 7 8 9 0

DEDICATION

This book is dedicated to those corporations with vision who are accepting their role as leaders, and as powerful resources of human energy and money, to effect social change and raise the quality of lives in countries around the world. Their decisions, based on an awareness of global ethical responsibility, can positively affect our basic problems of hunger and poverty, the environment, and the lives of children.

TABLE OF CONTENTS

LIST OF TABLES

PREFACE

This book has been written to assist Western firms and individual entrepreneurs crack the virgin marketplace in the Pacific Rim. In addition to the well-established trade centers of Hong Kong and Japan, this book covers the "Four Tigers" of the 1980s (Korea, Malaysia, Singapore, and Taiwan), the "New Tigers" of the 1990s (Indonesia and Thailand), and lastly, the Philippines.

The Introduction provides a regional overview, comparing and contrasting the individual country situations and highlighting a few of the common themes to be encountered.

In the chapters that follow, each country is profiled separately. The same basic topical outline is covered for each country, covering: historic and geographical context; socioeconomic and market demographics; politics and finance; policies to attract business; and important contacts and statistics. A map and key points are also included for each country.

The book concludes with a listing of key business contacts for the region, including U.S. government and multilateral resources. A comprehensive listing of trade shows follows. Finally, an exhaustive compendium of useful statistics is provided in the Appendix.

INTRODUCTION

INSIDER TRADING

All of the major Pacific Rim business cultures make a sharp distinction between "insiders" and "outsiders" — and they do not do business with outsiders. The solution is to become an insider by spending enough time and resources to build a solid personal relationship before starting with concrete proposals or negotiations. First, it is important for Americans to research potential business associates before entering another country. This includes a survey of how a particular target company conducts business and with whom. Second, it is not usually productive to start negotiations at the top of the organization. Often, initiating a relationship with mid-level management and building an internal coalition is the most productive route. Simultaneous discussions at several levels in the hierarchy (and in some cases, geographic diversity) are advised. This may require several trips and a sizeable amount of time, but that is the cost of doing business.

An excellent mechanism for becoming an insider is through the introduction of a respected third party. This may include a mutual business acquaintance, a law firm, trading company or association, government official, or a personal friend.

BREAK ON THROUGH TO THE OTHER SIDE

A corollary to the principle of achieving insider status is that the official and corporate bureaucracy can make life either miserable or divine. In Korea, Japan,

China, India, and many other Pacific Rim countries, red tape and economic nationalism can appear arbitrary and overly burdensome for Americans used to transparency in regulations and "equal access." The best solution to this dilemma is to select a local partner with powerful connections in key sectors of the appropriate bureaucracy. Otherwise, one must resort to the time-consuming process of becoming an insider. Either way, success will only come with patience and perseverance.

The notable exceptions in this realm are Hong Kong and Singapore. Both countries have an official bureaucracy considered the epitome of efficiency and professionalism, and both have a regulatory regime which is pared to the bone.

ONE PERSON'S CEILING IS ANOTHER PERSON'S FLOOR

Over the past two decades, Americans have adopted the popular view that negotiations will be most successful in a "win/win" scenario — achieving a middle ground through compromise and mutual cooperation. Unfortunately, this concept only works if everyone's singing from the same libretto. Generally, negotiators in the Pacific Rim — particularly in Japan, Korea, and China — will only accord "fairness" to other insiders or equals. If negotiating as an outsider, be on your guard, and be prepared to walk away from ludicrous situations. Negotiations can always be reinitiated when a better negotiating position has been achieved.

Most American business people that have business experience with the Japanese, for example, have doubtlessly observed that they bring large delegations to the negotiating table. Whenever possible, determine well in advance who will attend such a meeting, whether it is a formal negotiation, sales proposal, or even a courtesy call. Do the amount of homework necessary to understand who the players are and what their likely objectives might be. Commence "bilateral" lobbying prior to the actual meeting. This will require assembling a team of your own or running the risk of being outgunned by sheer numbers.

THE PEOPLE'S COURT

The American business style bestows enormous importance upon contractual agreements, typically drafted by lawyers trained to anticipate all of the possible "worst-case" scenarios as a safeguard to their clients. When difficulties in the business transactions arise, the contract is consulted and appropriate actions derived — including, of course, litigation in court. Relative to other cultures in the Pacific Rim,

Americans are extraordinarily litigious, and most businesses do not view litigation as diminishing their honor, reputation, or standing in the community.

In the Pacific Rim, the business style is to first build relationships with small transactions or ventures, and then broaden the scope over time. Generally, resorting to litigation to resolve a business dispute will not only end any hope of a continuance of business activities between the litigants, it will probably also diminish the prospects of establishing a relationship with another party — for fear of a similarly unpleasant outcome.

CRACKING THE PACIFIC RIM

CHAPTER ONE

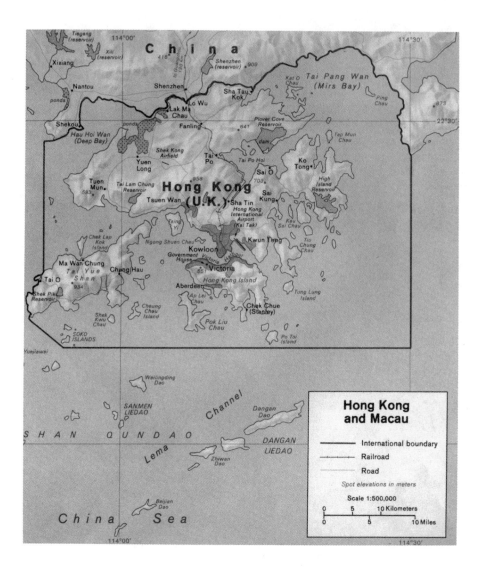

HONG KONG

HONG KONG

In a Nutshell

		Urban Population
Population (1992)	5,759,990	92.8%

Description of Area		Percentage of Total
Grass and Shrub	520 square kilometers	48.4
Woodlands	221 square kilometers	20.6
Residential	39 square kilometers	3.6
Vacant Development Land	34 square kilometers	3.2
Government	15 square kilometers	1.4
Open Space	14 square kilometers	1.3
Commercial	1 square kilometer	0.1

Land Area	398 square miles 1,040 square kilometers
Comparable European State	Slightly less than half the size of Luxembourg
Comparable U.S. State	Slightly less than six times the size of Washington, D.C.
Language	Chinese (Cantonese), English
Common Business Language	English
Currency	Hong Kong dollar (HK$ = 100 cents)
Best Air Connection	San Francisco-Hong Kong Daily nonstop: Singapore Air 800/742-3333 Los Angeles-Hong Kong Daily nonstop: Cathay Pacific 800/233-2742
Best Hotel	Grand Hyatt ($350/night as of 2/92)

CHAPTER CONTENTS

INTRODUCTION AND REGIONAL ORIENTATION

Geographical and Historical Background

Hong Kong lies at the southeastern tip of China, adjoining the province of Guangdong, and is south of the tropic of Cancer. The total land area of Hong Kong is 1,070 square kilometers. Described by Lord Palmerston as a "barren rock" when the British flag was first planted in Hong Kong in 1841, the Crown Colony nevertheless quickly became an important trading post and a gateway to China. By the end of the 19th century, the tip of the Kowloon Peninsula had also been ceded, and the New Territories were leased for 99 years to the British. Upon expiry of this term in 1997, sovereignty of Hong Kong will revert to China.

Hong Kong's traditional optimism was badly shaken by the brutal assault on Tiananmen Square and the subsequent crackdown throughout China in 1989. The PRC government's commitment to preserve Hong Kong was questioned following these events. Nevertheless, Hong Kong's unique location at the hub of Asia has increased its role as a great international trading port, a powerful manufacturing base, and the world's third largest financial center.

Demographics

Socioeconomic Indicators and Conditions

At the end of 1990, there were 5,812,300 people in Hong Kong, comprised of 2,968,500 males and 2,343,800 females. The growth rate of the population averaged 1.5% over the ten-year period, with fluctuations mainly due to changes in migration flows. The age distribution of the population has changed considerably in the last ten years. In 1979, 26.7% of the population was under 15; in 1989 the figure was 21.8%. The proportion of people aged 65 and above has risen from 6.2% to 8.5%.

Hong Kong is currently undergoing a test of confidence over the 1997 transition, particularly in light of the suppression of the prodemocracy movement in China in 1989. Many Hong Kong residents have chosen to relocate. The brain drain phenomenon is now a fact of life and business in Hong Kong. An estimated 55,000 Hong Kong residents will emigrate in 1990. Recent studies have indicated that nearly half of all Hong Kong professionals intend to leave before 1997.

Trends in Consumer Demand

In 1989 total imports grew 9% in real terms to $72.2 billion. Hong Kong recorded a trade surplus of $991 million in 1989 against a $734 million deficit in 1988.

However, it is anticipated that the domestic demand will drop due to the prodemocracy movement in China.

Political/Institutional Infrastructure

Hong Kong is administered by the Hong Kong government, which is developed from the basic pattern applied in all British-governed territories overseas. The head of Hong Kong government is the Governor. Under the terms of the "Joint Declaration of the British and Chinese Governments on the Question of Hong Kong" which entered into force on May 27, 1985, Hong Kong will become, effective July 1, 1997, a Special Administrative Region of the People's Republic of China.

The Governor has the ultimate direction of the administration of Hong Kong. He is advised on the development of policy and other matters by an Executive Council. Members of the Legislative Council provide funds, enact legislation, debate policy, and question the administration. Two municipal councils, the Urban Council and the Regional Council, have a statutory responsibility to provide public health, cultural activities, and recreational services in their respective areas. In addition, 19 District Boards cover the territory, advising on the implementation of policies at district level and providing an effective forum for public consultation.

Political Organization

Governor. As head of the government, he presides at meetings of both the Executive Council and the Legislative Council. He is also the representative of the Queen in Hong Kong.

Executive Council. This group consists of four ex-officio members — the Chief Secretary, the Commander British Forces, the Financial Secretary, and the Attorney General — together with other members who are appointed by the Governor with the approval of the Secretary of State.

Legislative Council. Constituted by virtue of the Letters Paten, its primary function is the enactment of legislation, including legislation for the appropriation of public funds.

Finance Committee. It consists of the Chief Secretary, the Financial Secretary, one official member of the Council, and all members other than official members.

Public Accounts Committee. This is a standing committee consisting of a chairman and six members, none of whom is an official member of the council.

Select Committees. Its function is to enable small groups of members to examine complex problems, usually by taking evidence and reporting their findings and recommendations to the council.

OMELCO. This stands for Office of the Members of the Executive and Legislative Councils.

Urban Council. This is a statutory council with responsibilities for the provision of municipal services.

Regional Council. This council is the statutory municipal authority for the New Territories.

Trade Flows

Top Import/Export Trade Partners

The top six export trade partners for Hong Kong are: the United States, China, EEC, Federal Republic of Germany, United Kingdom, and Japan. The top six import trade partners are: China, Japan, EEC, Taiwan, United States, and Korea.

Top Import/Export Commodities

The top seven export commodities include: articles of apparel and clothing accessories, watches and clocks, electrical machinery, apparatus and appliances, textiles, electronic components, and parts for computers. The top four imported commodities include: raw materials, consumer goods, capital goods, and foodstuffs.

Finance and Investment Policies

The Hong Kong government pursues a policy of minimum interference in corporate initiative. This applies to trade in goods and services as well as to industrial investment. Hong Kong welcomes foreign investment, both for additional capital and for its introduction of new, improved production technologies and processes. The government makes no distinction in law or practice between investments by foreign-controlled companies and those of local interests.

There are no specific regulations governing investments nor are there specific screening requirements, except for regulations imposed on financial and insurance institutions. The government has begun to follow a modified industrial land policy to ensure that scarcity of land does not deter newer industrial development, particularly in the New Territories. There are no laws per se regulating acquisition and takeover activities. The legal system in Hong Kong makes no distinction between local and foreign corporations. Commercial and company law provide for effective enforcement of contracts and protection of corporate rights.

Policies to Attract New Business

Preferred Foreign Investment Projects

There is no specific legislation designed to attract foreign investors nor are there laws to protect or subsidize domestic industries.

Investment Incentives and Privileges

Hong Kong offers no special privileges for foreign investors nor does it protect or subsidize domestic industries or exports. The government imposes no export performance or local content requirements.

Tax Incentives

There are no capital gains taxes or withholding taxes on dividends or royalties. For tax purposes, deductions are allowed for the costs of patents, legal expenses incurred in borrowings, and capital expenditures for construction of buildings and structures and for machinery and equipment.

Free Trade Zones/Special Economic Zones

Hong Kong is a free port.

APPROACHING THE MARKET

Foreign Trade and Investment Decision-Making Structure

Slackening demand in some of Hong Kong's major markets, notably the United States, slowed growth in domestic exports, but Hong Kong's rapid development as a service and sourcing center for the region was evidenced by a 25.8% growth in re-export. The manufacturing sector still plays a vital role in Hong Kong's growth. The value of manufactured exports rose by 3% to $223,104 million during the year, demonstrating that Hong Kong's economy remains basically sound, and its manufactured products remain competitive in major overseas markets.

It is estimated that up to 90% of Hong Kong's manufacturing output is eventually exported. The lack of natural resources and the limited supply of land for industrial use have generally constrained diversification into capital and land-intensive industries. Light manufacturing industries that produce mainly consumer goods predominate. Textiles, clothing, electronics, watches and clocks, and plastics are the major industries, together accounting for 66% of Hong Kong's total manufacturing employment and 71% of total domestic exports in 1989.

State and Private Services

Credit Survey

The Hong Kong Export Credit Insurance Corporation (ECIC) is a member of the International Union of Credit and Investment Insurers (The Berne Union). It has regular access to confidential and updated economic and market information on all major trading countries.

Being a professional credit manager itself, the corporation conducts credibility assessments of overseas buyers and gives advice on credit-risks monitoring and debt collection. These services prove invaluable to exporters lacking the resources of effective credit management systems. The corporation has a computerized databank containing information on over 60,000 overseas buyers.

Incorporation/Registration

The Companies Registry of the Registrar General's Department keeps records of all companies incorporated in Hong Kong and of all overseas companies that have established a place of business in Hong Kong. On incorporation, a company pays a registration fee of $600 plus $6 for every $1,000 of nominal capital. Companies incorporated overseas are required to register certain documents with the registry within one month of establishing a place of business in Hong Kong. The registry also deals with the incorporation of trustees under the Registered Trustees Incorporation Ordinance and with the registration of limited partnerships.

Setting Up Business Operations

Sales Promotion, Fairs, and Conferences

The Hong Kong Trade Development Council (HKTDC) is a statutory body responsible for promoting and developing Hong Kong's overseas trade and publicizing the opportunities and advantages of Hong Kong as a trading partner. Council staff carried out an extensive trade promotion program in 1989, organizing more than 80 major international projects. The council produces eight magazines and a newspaper for general circulation and distribution at trade events around the world.

Consignment and Re-Export

Re-exports showed a significant increase in 1989, accounting for 61% of the combined total of domestic exports and re-exports. Principal commodities re-exported were: textiles ($42,529 million); miscellaneous manufactured articles ($42,359 million); clothing ($37,281); electrical machinery, apparatus, and appliances ($33,550 million); telecommunications, sound recording, and reproducing apparatus and equipment ($27,552 million), as well as photographic apparatus, equipment, supplies, and optical goods, watches and clocks ($13,485 million). The main origins of these re-exports were China, Japan, the United States, Taiwan, and the Republic of Korea. Largest re-export markets were China, the United States, Japan, Taiwan, and the Republic of Korea.

Transportation and Freight (Air/Sea)

As one of the world's leading maritime centers, Hong Kong shipowners control over 50 million deadweight tons, making them a global force. Hong Kong moves more container tonnage by far than any other single port in the world.

Hong Kong has the second busiest international airport. Serviced by more than 30 foreign carriers, Hong Kong International Airport boasts excellent passenger and cargo facilities. It will soon have a new tow runway, operating 24-hours.

INVESTMENT CLIMATE

Privatization, Investment Protection, and Dispute Settlement

Hong Kong offers no special privileges for foreign investors nor does it protect or subsidize domestic industries or exports. The government imposes no export performance or local content requirements.

Local laws provide adequate avenues and effective legal recourse for investors. The Hong Kong Industry Department is available to help solve any problems related to foreign investment.

Hong Kong has steadily liberalized its telecommunications sector. A U.S.-backed consortium won the franchise to offer cable television to Hong Kong audiences. Construction has started to build a network of cables and fibers able to transmit data. Thus, the provision of private data and voice networks — if government liberalization continues along the same path — may offer excellent opportunities.

The inducements for investment in Hong Kong include an established code of commercial law, excellent communications and transportation links, enforced protection for intellectual property, and government policies for free and open trade and investment.

Joint Ventures and Wholly Owned Subsidiaries

Foreign and domestically-owned companies are allowed to set up offices, incorporate, and register branches and subsidiaries without strict government guidelines defining the future scope of their activities or mandating levels of performance. Companies may be structured without onerous conditions regarding ownership, management, and composition of boards. There is no quota system governing foreign investment, staffing, or management of foreign-owned operations.

Taxation and Regulatory Conditions

Sources of Income Liable to Taxation

In Hong Kong, persons liable to tax may be assessed on three separate and distinct sources of income: business profits, salaries, and income from property.

Company Tax

Foreign and domestically-owned firms are taxed at the same rate. The corporate profit tax rate in Hong Kong is currently 16.5% per annum, one of the lowest in the region. There is no withholding tax on dividends paid by corporations, and dividends received from corporations are exempt from profits tax.

Personal Income Tax

Salaries tax is charged on emoluments arising in or derived from Hong Kong. The basis of assessment and the payment method are similar to the system for profit tax. Tax payable is calculated on a sliding scale progressing from 3% to 21% at multiples of 3% on the first seven segments of net income of $10,000 each and then to 25% on the remaining net income.

Property Tax

The owner of land or buildings in Hong Kong is charged property tax at the standard rate of 15% on the actual rent received, less an allowance of 20% for repairs and maintenance. Property owned by a corporation carrying on a business in Hong Kong is exempt from property tax, but the profits derived from the ownership are chargeable to profits tax.

Estate Duty

Estate duty is imposed on estates in Hong Kong. The rates of duty charge from a minimum of 6% on estates valued between $2 million and $2.5 million to a maximum of 18% on estates valued in excess of $5 million. Estates valued at less than $2 million are exempt from duty.

Insurance

Hong Kong has some of the most liberal rules in the world for establishment of foreign insurance companies. This factor, plus rising per capita income and the expanding middle class need for group insurance, has spurred an industry which boasts 273 authorized companies at the beginning of 1990. In contrast there are only six or seven true competitors. Life insurance sales performed best in the late 1980s, a trend expected to continue with expansion.

FINANCING AND CAPITAL MARKETS

Banking and Other Financial Institutions

Since 1981, deposit-taking institutions in Hong Kong have been classified into three separate groups: licensed banks, licensed deposit-taking companies, and registered deposit-taking companies.

At the end of 1989, there were 165 licensed banks in Hong Kong, 31 of which were locally incorporated. They maintained a total of 1,542 offices in Hong Kong. In addition, there were 158 representative offices of foreign banks.

Only licensed banks may operate current or savings accounts. Licensed deposit-taking company status is granted at the discretion of the Financial Secretary. Companies are required to have a minimum issued share capital of $100 million and paid-up capital of $75 million and to meet certain criteria regarding size, ownership, and quality of management.

Tapping International Aid Institutions

Hong Kong enjoys a relatively high per capital GDP and its investment climate is favorable. There is no active OPIC program in the territory.

Financial Market Operations

Money Market

Hong Kong has a mature and active foreign exchange market, forming an integral part of the corresponding global market. The link with other major overseas centers enables foreign exchange dealing to continue 24 hours a day around the globe. Equally well-established and active is the interbank money market, in which wholesale Hong Kong dollar deposits and foreign currency deposits are traded both between deposit-taking institutions in Hong Kong and between local and overseas institutions. This market is mainly for short-term money — from maturities ranging from overnight to six months for Hong Kong dollars and to 12 months for U.S. dollars.

Securities Market

The stock market constitutes another important source of capital for local enterprises, attracting interest from both local and overseas investors. At the end of 1989, 298 public companies, with a total market capitalization of $605 billion, were listed on the Hong Kong Stock Exchange, making it the fourth-largest stock market in Asia after Japan, Taiwan, and South Korea. The average turnover in 1989 was $1,216 million.

Gold Market

The Chinese Gold and Silver Exchange Society operates one of the fourth largest gold bullion markets in the world. Gold traded through the society is of 99% fineness, weighed in taels and quoted in Hong Kong dollars. After allowing for exchange rate fluctuations, prices closely follow those of the major markets in London, Zurich, and New York.

There is another active gold market in Hong Kong, known as the loco-London gold market. The main participants are banks, major international bullion houses, and gold-trading companies. Prices are quoted in U.S. dollars per troy ounces of gold of 99.95% fineness and delivery is in London. Trading in this market has grown significantly in recent years.

Futures Market

The Hong Kong Futures Exchange offers contracts in sugar, soybeans, gold, and Hang Seng Index futures. The Exchange is making special efforts to establish itself as an effective self-regulatory organization, the front-line regulator in a two-tier regulatory regime as recommended by the Securities Review Committee.

LICENSING, PATENTS, AND TRADEMARKS

Trademark, Patent, and Copyright Protection

Hong Kong has acceded to the Paris Convention for the Protection of Industrial Property, the Berne International Copyright Convention, and the Geneva and Paris Universal Copyright Convention. To meet convention obligations, Hong Kong has developed comprehensive laws covering trademarks, trade descriptions, copyrights, industrial designs, and patents. Hong Kong has no intellectual property laws or administrative practices hindering trade. Overall, the territory has a solid reputation as a protector and enforcer of intellectual property rights.

Trademarks are registered under the Trade Marks Ordinance, the provisions of which are similar to trade marks legislation in the United Kingdom. The procedure in applying for registration is laid down in the Trade Marks Rules, and the prescribed forms may be obtained free from the Trade Marks Registry.

VISITING AND LOCATING

General Travel Checklist

Visas

Visitors must hold a valid passport, endorsed where necessary for Hong Kong. Citizens of some 22 countries, including the USA and certain Western European and South American nations, are permitted one-month visa-free visits. Three-month visa-free visits are available to another 24 countries. (The British are allowed a six-month no-visa stay.) Check your status at any British Consulate, High Commission, or Visa office before you depart.

Currency

The unit of currency is the Hong Kong dollar (HK$). Notes are issued by The Hong Kong and Shanghai Banking Corporation and the Standard Chartered Bank in denominations of HK $1,000, HK $500, HK $50, HK $20, and HK $10. There are silver coins for HK $5, HK $2, and HK $1, and bronze coins for HK 50c and HK 10c. Since October 17, 1983, the Hong Kong dollar has been linked to the U.S. dollar, through an arrangement in the note-issue mechanism, at a fixed rate of HK $7.80 = US $1.

Most foreign currencies and traveler's checks are easily changed in Hong Kong, either at banks, hotels, or money-changers. American Express® cardholders now have access to Jetco automated teller machines (ATM) and can withdraw local currency and traveler's checks at Express Cash® ATMs. Holders of Visa® cards can also obtain local currency from the Hong Kong Bank "Electronic Money" ATM at the airport and eight other convenient locations.

Getting Around

Public transportation is efficient and inexpensive, although very busy on weekends, public holidays, and during peak travel times. The air-conditioned Airbus service operates between Hong Kong International Airport and most major hotels. Taxis are numerous and readily available. Red taxis serve Hong Kong Island and Kowloon; green ones in the New Territories and blue ones on Lantau Island operate at lower rates. Double-decker buses, which run from 6:00 a.m. until midnight, cover most parts of the territory. The Kowloon-Canton Railway runs 34 kilometers from Hung Hom in Kowloon up to the border with China. The Mass Transit Railway, Hong Kong's fast, efficient, and air-conditioned underground system, runs not only along the north side of Hong Kong Island, but also from central across the harbor dividing into east and west branches in Kowloon.

Accommodations and Housing

Almost every major international hotel chain is represented in Hong Kong, the home base for many world-renowned hotel groups. The daily rates range between US $20 (HK $156) and US $2,600 (HK $20,000). For those who plan to stay in Hong Kong on a long-term basis, a wide selection of apartments and houses is available. Rental costs vary considerably, depending on location and size.

Electricity Supply

The voltage in Hong Kong is 200 volts, 50 cycles. Most hotels provide adapters.

Telecom, Postal, and Courier Services

Local calls are free, although some hotels charge a handling fee. Public phones cost HK $1. Long-distance calls can be made from International Direct Dialing (IDD) public coin phones; from Cable and Wireless offices; and by Cardphone (IDD only). A push-button, call-home direct service, which connects the caller with the operator in his or her own country on a collect-call basis, is also available. The service extends to nine countries and is offered at nine locations including the airport.

The main post offices on Hong Kong Island (next to the Star Ferry) and in Kowloon (between Jordan and Yau Ma Tei MTR stations) are open from 8:00 a.m. to 6:00 p.m. Mondays to Saturdays.

Business Cards

Formal business introduction in Hong Kong needs an exchange of business cards. It is advisable for foreign visitors to have their cards printed in both English and Chinese (Cantonese).

Business Hours

Most offices open from 9:00 a.m. to 5:00 p.m. with a lunch hour from 1:00 p.m. to 2:00 p.m. On Saturdays the hours are 9:00 a.m. to 1:00 p.m. Many Chinese businesses open at 10:00 a.m. and close around 6:00 p.m. Major banks are open from 9:00 a.m. to 4:30 p.m. on weekdays, 9:00 a.m. to 12:30 p.m. on Saturdays.

Tipping

Most restaurants add 10% service charge automatically; however, an additional 5% is expected. Small tips are expected for taxi drivers, bellboys, doormen, and washroom attendants.

What to Wear

Hong Kong's climate is subtropical, tending towards temperate for nearly half the year. During November and December there are pleasant breezes, plenty of sunshine, and comfortable temperatures. Many people regard these as the best months of the year. Light clothing is essential, although a jacket and sweater are necessary in winter months when the temperature can drop to $0°C$. About 80% of the rain falls between May and September.

Health Care

All water direct from government mains in Hong Kong satisfies the United Nations World Health Organization standards. Bottled water is widely available in hotels and supermarkets.

There are 5,512 doctors registered on the local list of the Hong Kong Medical Council. The majority of doctors and dentists speak good English.

The Media

There are two English channels. Programming includes a selection of locally produced items plus features from Britain, the USA, and Australia.

Three English-language channels provide a wide range of programs. The BBC World Service is also relayed at certain times of the day.

Availability of Foreign Products

Because Hong Kong is a free port, a diversified variety of foreign products can be purchased.

Shopping

In terms of value, variety, and services, Hong Kong offers some of the best shopping in the world. Not only can you find a spectacular selection of arts and crafts from all over China and the Orient, but also brand-name products from around the world. The range of shopping places is extensive; it includes malls and hotel arcades, shopping complexes, department stores, boutiques, markets, and street stalls. Hong Kong offers an infinite choice of shopping in a conveniently compact area and excellent value for money as well.

Obtain a copy of the Hong Kong Tourist Association's (HKTA) shopping guide, available free of charge only at HKTA Information and Gift Centers in Hong Kong. This contains listings of all HKTA member outlets with maps pinpointing their locations, useful advice on buying specific items, size charts — in fact, everything you need to know about shopping in Hong Kong.

Dining Out

Hong Kong is truly a gourmet's paradise, offering the best Chinese food in the world. Specialties from all of the neighboring Asian countries and superb Western cuisine is also available.

Dining out is a way of life here: Hong Kong's 19,000 eating establishments are full at breakfast, lunch, or dinner time. The HKTA's Dining and Nightlife guide, available free of charge at HKTA Information and Gift Centers in Hong Kong, is a must for visitors. It describes the regional cuisines of China, suggests dishes to try, and gives reviews of all HKTA member restaurants.

Entertainment

Hong Kong's deluxe or first-class hotels have fine restaurants and lounge bars, ranging in style from sophisticated intimacy to palatial grandeur. Hong Kong has a wide range of drinking spots — from luxurious oak-panelled lounges to casual drinking dives — all with their own decor theme. As in every other category of nightlife, the visitor has a wide choice, from Western-style dinner-dance restaurants and casual Chinese nightclubs, to luxuriously decorated cabaret restaurants with full Chinese floor shows. Hong Kong's jet-set discos are equal to those anywhere in the world, with the latest disco and video hits, as well as the most up-to-date sound and light effects. Most are located in hotels and are packed on Fridays, Saturdays, and eves of public holidays, when premium charges apply.

Sightseeing and Tourist Information

Hong Kong offers the tourist more sights and attractions per square kilometer than anywhere else in the world. A whole spectrum of places can be seen — from traditional Chinese temples and old walled villages, to the rural scene with its farms, mountains, rivers and country parts, to the beauty of the 235 outlying islands, to the many different areas of the bustling, dynamic metropolis.

One of the best ways to explore Hong Kong is on foot. The HKTA publishes the Central and Western District Walking Tour, the Yau Ma Tei Walking Tour, and the Cheung Chau Walking Tour providing detailed route maps and background information on points of interest along the way.

Recreational Opportunities

With the completion of more recreational facilities, the people of Hong Kong have a wider choice as to how to spend their leisure time. A large number participate in or watch the many regularly-held sporting events. Others spend their weekends in the countryside, on beaches, or in swimming pools.

Despite Hong Kong's largely urban environment, opportunities for sport and recreation are not lacking in the territory. No place is far from green countryside and there are 21 country parks covering over 40% of the total land area.

The Expatriate

The Immigration Department is responsible for controlling the entry of foreign workers for employment in Hong Kong. Generally speaking, foreigners possessing special skills or experience not readily available in Hong Kong are allowed entry. Those able to contribute substantially to the economic well-being of Hong Kong, including bankers, entrepreneurs, and other persons whose activities are likely to stimulate local employment, are considered for entry. In all cases, normal immigration requirements must be met. The Immigration Department considers special cases in consultation with the Labor Department and other expert departments.

Entry and departure from Hong Kong for business travel and tourism is minimally restricted for American citizens. Visas allowing residence and local employment for expatriates are granted on the basis of simple, comprehensible procedures handled in a timely manner, not subject to onerous restrictions, and managed in a way that is consistent with the interests of employers. Expatriates residing in Hong Kong enjoy a wide variety of amenities and advantages making the territory the most desirable venue for foreign companies to base their Asian operations.

The labor force. Hong Kong's labor market continues to be very tight due to a high level of economic activity. The brain drain problem, due to emigration of professionals and experienced personnel, continues to cause concern. Employers are adopting new approaches to tackle the problem of staff recruitment and retention. Unemployment for the third quarter of 1989 was at a low of 1.4%, and underemployment was 0.6%. According to the 1989 General Household Surveys, Hong Kong's dynamic workforce totalled 2.8 million, 64% males and 36% females.

Employment and labor relations. In 1989, the Labor Relations Service of the Labor Department conciliated in 130 trade disputes leading to seven work stoppages, with a loss of 3,270 working days. To promote good labor-management relations, a committee on labor relations was set up in 1986 by the Labor Advisory Board.

Conditions of work. The Employment of Children Regulations, made under the Employment Ordinance, prohibits the employment of children under 15 in any industrial undertakings. Under the Women and Young Persons Regulations, young persons aged 15 to 17 and women are permitted to work eight hours a day and six days a week in industry. Their working hours may exceed eight on one or more days in any week or 48 hours in a week. In industry, overtime employment for women is restricted to two hours a day and 200 hours a year, while persons under the age of 18 are not permitted to work overtime.

HONG KONG

KEY CONTACTS

American Embassy Contacts

American Embassy Hong Kong
26 Garden Road
Box 30
FPO San Francisco 96659-0002
Tel: 852/5-239011
Fax: 852/5-845-1598
Telex: 63141 USDOC HX

Consul General:	Richard L. Williams
Deputy Principal Officer:	David G. Brown
Political/Economic Section:	Gilbert J. Donahue
Commercial Section:	Ying Price
Consul (Consular Section):	John H. Adams
Immigration and Naturalization Officer:	Jerry W. Stuchiner
Administrative Section:	J. Michael O'Brien
Regional Security Officer:	John H. Kaufmann
Agricultural Section:	Phillip C. Holloway
Public Affairs Officer:	Lloyd W. Neighbors
Customs Service:	Thomas E. Gray
Office of the Defense Attache:	Capt. John W. Athanson, U.S.N.

Business Contacts

British Embassy
Peter Lo, Minister to Washington
Hong Kong Trade Section
1233 20th Street, NW #504
Washington, DC 20036
Tel: 202/331-8947
Fax: 202/331-8958

Hong Kong Economic Affairs Office
126 East 56th Street, 14th Floor
New York, NY 10022
    Tel: 212/355-4060

Hong Kong Economic Affairs
Industrial Promotion Office
180 Sutter Street
San Francisco, CA 94104
    Tel: 415/956-4560

Hong Kong Trade Development Council
World Trade Center
350 South Figueroa Street #520
Los Angeles, CA 90071
    Tel: 213/622-3194

Hong Kong Government Industrial Promotion Office

New York:
548 5th Avenue
New York, NY 10036
    Tel: 212/730-0777

Chicago:
333 North Michigan Avenue
Suite 2028
Chicago, IL 60601
    Tel: 312/726-4515

Dallas:
PO Box 58329
Dallas, TX 75258
    Tel: 214/748-8162

American Chamber of Commerce in Hong Kong
1030 Swire House
Hong Kong
    Cable: AMCHAM
    Telex: 83664 AMCC HX

The Hong Kong General Chamber of Commerce
United Centre, 22d Floor
95 Queensway
P.O. Box 852
Hong Kong

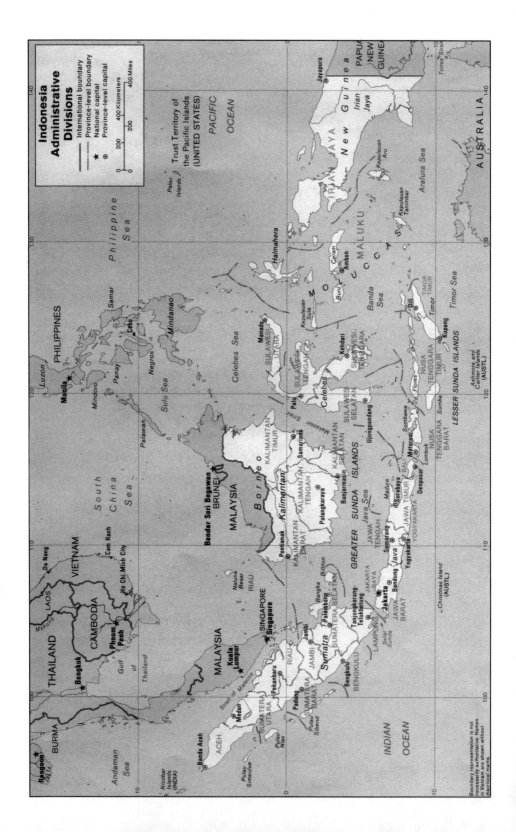

INDONESIA

INDONESIA

In a Nutshell

		Urban Population
Population (1992)	181,400,000	27.1%

Main Urban Areas		Percentage of Total
Jakarta	7,636,000	4.2
Surabaya	2,289,000	1.2
Bandung	1,602,000	0.8
Medan	1,966,000	1.1
Semarang	1,269,000	0.6

Land Area	735,268 square miles 1,904,344 square kilometers
Comparable European State	Slightly more than three times the size of France
Comparable U.S. State	Slightly more than three times the size of Texas
Language	Bahasa Indonesia (official), English, and Dutch
Common Business Language	English
Currency	Indonesian rupiah (1Rp = 100 sen)
Best Air Connection	Los Angeles-Honolulu-Biak-Bali-Jakarta Garuda Indonesian Airlines 800/342-7832
Best Hotel	Grand Hyatt ($250/night as of 2/92)

CHAPTER CONTENTS

INTRODUCTION AND REGIONAL ORIENTATION

Geographical and Historical Background

Indonesia is an archipelagic country composed of 13,677 islands, covering an area of 7,776 square kilometers. The total land area is 1,904,344 square kilometers. Java, Sumatra, Kalimanan (Borneo), Sulawesi (Celebes), Irian Jaya, and Bali are the principal islands. Jakarta, the capital and major port, is located on Java. Surabaya, the second largest city and port, is located on eastern Java. The island of Sumatra contains 20% of the total population, and Belawan, the third largest port. Indonesia is divided into 27 provinces, which are further divided into 246 districts and 55 municipalities.

Demographics

Socioeconomic Indicators and Conditions

With 180 million inhabitants, Indonesia is the fifth most populous country in the world. Sixty percent of the population is located on the island of Java. Eighty percent of the population is Muslim; the remainder are mostly Buddhist and Christian. There are over 300 ethnic groups. While the Chinese comprise only 5% of the population, they own 19 out of every 20 businesses. Adult literacy is approximately 62%, while primary school enrollment is 86%.

Political/Institutional Infrastructure

President Soeharto, who took power in a coup in 1965, is the overwhelmingly dominant figure in the Indonesian political system. The political system is based on the 1945 constitution which provides for limited separation of executive, legislative, and judicial powers. General elections are held every five years to choose the 1,000 member People's Consultative Assembly (MPR), which then elects the president and vice-president to five-year terms.

The Indonesian policy is an authoritarian system. Military officers, both active and retired, fill large numbers of posts as key advisers and members of the bureaucracy. The lack of political openness is justified by the need for economic development. The central government is dominated by the Javanese.

In addition to the People's Consultative Assembly, the legislative branch also includes the 500-member House of Representatives (DPR). The judicial system is capped by the Supreme Court. Under the 1945 constitution, two other government bodies are considered branches of government on the same level as the executive, legislative, and judicial branches — the Supreme Audit Board (BPK) and the Supreme Advisory Council (DPA). The BPK examines government accounts, and the DPA advises the president on matters of state.

The ideological foundation of the state and community life is "pancasila." The term is described as "the five inseparable and mutually qualifying principles of Belief in the One Supreme God, a Just and Civilized Humanity, the Unity of Indonesia, a Democracy Guided by the Inner Wisdom of Consultation-Representation, and Social Justice for All."

Political Party

The three political parties in Indonesia are the Golkar (functional groups), Indonesian Democracy party (PDI), and the United Development party (PPP).

Trade Flows

Top 10 Import/Export Trade Partners

The import market share for 1988 was as follows:

• Japan	30.8%
• West Germany	26.9%
• France	16.2%
• United States	7.8%
• Taiwan	4.1%
• Singapore	2.3%
• United Kingdom	1.8%
• Netherlands	1.6%
• Hong Kong	1.3%
• Switzerland	1.1%

Top 10 Import/Export Commodities

Major imports for 1988 included: machinery and transport equipment, petroleum, chemicals, and iron and steel products. Major exports for 1988 included: petroleum, plywood, rubber, liquefied natural gas, coffee, nickel ore, bauxite, and coal.

Finance and Investment Policies

Indonesia is the economic giant of ASEAN and has been attracting massive investments, estimated at $70 billion from 1989 to 1991. U.S. private investments have grown from less than $1 billion to about $2 billion by year-end 1991. ASEAN is the Association of Southeast Asian Nations, established in 1967. The six members are: Brunei, Indonesia, Malaysia, Philippines, Singapore, and Thailand.

As part of the Indonesian government's deregulation program, rules and procedures governing foreign investment have undergone extensive simplification and streamlining since 1985. This has included the simplification and rationalization of licensing and control procedures, the opening of certain areas previously off-limits to the private sector, reductions in import tariffs and the elimination of many nontariff barriers, the easing of joint venture and investment requirements, the improvement of the legal system in regard to intellectual property and recourse for contractual violations.

Policy priorities include infrastructure development, upgrading of human resources, and deregulation. Over 50 state-owned firms were scheduled for sale during 1990 to 1991. In November 1989, the Indonesian government authorized sales of equity in 52 state-owned enterprises. Public offerings were to begin in 1991, although the government plans to spread out sales over time in order to not disrupt the stock market. Sales of equity in public enterprises should lessen dependency on government financing in the long run.

In addition, the government announced that 59 other state-owned firms would undergo legal changes such as mergers or joint ventures, while 75 would have various steps taken to enhance their efficiency. In total, the November 1990 government's announcement affected 186 of the more than 210 state-owned enterprises. The government further attempted to ease restrictions on business by instituting reform measures ranging from improved customs clearance, reduction of licensing requirements, and changes in foreign ownership regulations. Certain sectors, such as communications, transport, and the retail trade, remain more restrictive to foreign investment.

Policies to Attract New Business

The Indonesian government has recently launched a program to loosen regulatory and administrative controls on the economy to improve the business climate and encourage foreign investment. The U.S. Commerce Department has entered into a "work agreement" with Indonesian telecommunications authorities to develop closer relationships leading to opportunities for the American telecommunications industry. The agreement has already led to considerable activity in trade missions and a feasibility study finding by the U.S. Trade and Development Program.

Investment Incentives and Privileges

The Indonesian government announced a massive deregulation package on May 28, 1990 which radically lowered tariffs and attempted to simplify market access. The package did the following:

- Lowered tariffs on 2,481 items.
- Eliminated quotas and nontariff barriers on 371 industrial projects, three pharmaceutical categories, and four commodities.
- Reduced import surcharges on 64 products and eliminated them on 53 products.
- Simplified licensing procedures and regulations for the pharmaceutical industry, thereby opening the market for new factories.
- Cut electronics tariffs for finished electronics producers from 60% to 40%.
- Simplified permits issued by the Department of Agriculture.

Tax Incentives

The Indonesian government eliminated tax holidays as an investment incentive in 1990, pointing to new tax legislation in 1986 as providing benefits during the entire life of the investment, instead of the initial start-up period. In practice, tax holidays were of little benefit in most investment cases. The 1986 tax law lowered the maximum tax rate to 35% for both individuals and businesses. The law also allowed more favorable declining balance depreciation provisions than the old law.

Other investment incentives introduced in 1989 to 1990 included full exemption from import duties and the stamp tax for all equipment and materials of construction needed to build and start operating the project, subject to control by monetary limit. Duties and taxes are also waived on raw materials needed for an initial production period, also controlled by monetary limit.

Certain personal necessities for expatriate personnel similarly enter tax and duty free. Foreign investors are supplied with a master list of capital goods, tools, and spare parts that may be imported duty free to start up a venture. This list usually excludes items deemed to be available locally, contributing to import substitution priority.

APPROACHING THE MARKET

Foreign Trade and Investment Decision-Making Infrastructure

The Indonesian market should be viewed as a long-term developmental target rather than an individual profit center, which has historically been characteristic of the view U.S. firms have taken. Successful foreign firms tend to view the Indonesian market within the context of a global market strategy.

Indonesia has a reputation as a difficult place to do business, in large part because its decision-making structure differs sharply from those found in Western countries. There is also a prevailing perception in Indonesia that U.S. firms are too short-run oriented and in some ways risky to do business with because they are not well supported by their home government relative to their European and Japanese competitors.

The Investment Coordinating Board (BKPM) was set up by the government as a one-stop center for approving foreign investment. There have been constant efforts to simplify procedures for processing investment applications, but flaws still exist. While BKPM was planned as a one-stop investment agency, most investors find it useful to maintain informal contacts with appropriate technical ministries as well.

Typical steps normally followed by a foreign company to successfully complete an investment project in Indonesia include the following:

- Select a joint venture partner and sign a joint venture agreement. This selection is extremely important as many ventures have turned sour because of differences between partners.
- Obtain a notarized incorporation in Indonesia (creating a "Perseroan Terbatas," P.T., company) and submit it to the Department of State.
- Submit an investment application to BKPM. Within four weeks, BKPM will issue a Provisional Letter of Approval (SPT) if the investment is in accordance with the priority list. Within six weeks of receipt of the additional information, BKPM will issue a Presidential Letter of Approval (SPT) under the terms of the Chairman's decree, along with a list of incentives granted and a temporary operating permit. The Department of Justice will issue its approval of the P.T. company.

State and Private Services

Market Research

While a growing number of Indonesian organizations engage in market research, it is sometimes difficult to find the level of competence required by Western firms. Branches of American banks in Jakarta make market surveys for their customers, and several U.S. consulting firms now have affiliates in Jakarta.

Market research in Indonesia is difficult because detailed statistics on production and consumption are often not available in published sources. External trade statistics are fairly detailed, and additional data may be obtained for a fee from the Central Bureau of Statistics (CBS), although unrecorded trade may distort import values and trends. In addition, CBS figures understate import values, since they exclude duty-free imports such as imports for investment and certain other transactions.

Indonesian consulting firms in Jakarta have formed the Association of Indonesian Consultants (IKINDO), whose members perform a wide range of research and consulting services. The address of the Association is Jl. Gondangdia Lama 23, Jakarta.

P.T. Data Consult, Ind., P.O. Box 108/JNG, Jakarta, publishes a newsletter twice monthly entitled "Indonesian Commercial Newsletter" containing a sectoral survey and other market information. Information and advice on other consulting and research firms that can undertake market surveys may be obtained from the Foreign Commercial Service (FCS), American Embassy, Jakarta.

Credit Survey

There are few reliable sources of formal reference and credit checks in Indonesia. Banks, advisory companies, the American Chamber of Commerce in Indonesia (AMCHAM), and the U.S. Embassy Foreign Commercial Service can provide some reference assistance. However, there is no alternative to establishing and cultivating direct personal contact in evaluating a potential partner and obtaining informed, soundly based advice on structuring an agreement.

Legal Services

Foreigners are barred from practicing law.

Setting Up Business Operations

No business transactions or decisions are completed quickly in Indonesia. Be prepared to spend a good deal of time with a client before getting down to the business transaction.

Developing rapport and friendship with prospects is crucial to concluding a transaction. Although the quality and prices of products are important, they are secondary to personal interaction.

While no new trade regulations should arise to hamper the trade environment, import restrictions may be issued for equipment similar to that being produced in Indonesia.

Only Indonesian companies are permitted to operate in the fields of importing and exporting and the wholesale and retail distribution of imported or locally produced goods in the domestic market. An Indonesian company is defined as one having 51% or more Indonesian ownership and a board of directors consisting mostly of Indonesian nationals.

An exception to this regulation is made for foreign investors engaged in production or manufacturing. They may import raw materials for their own use and export their own products. However, foreign investors are not permitted to undertake the distribution of their products in the local market. An investor frequently arranges to have a separate trading company owned by its local partner handle distribution. Domestic investors in production and manufacturing and some government agencies may also be permitted to import for their own use.

Forms of Business Organization

Limited liability company. "Perseroan Terbatas" (P.T.) is the only relevant type of business organization for most foreign investors. The legal characteristics of the P.T. are specified in Articles 36-56 of the Indonesian Commercial Code. A limited liability company may be formed by foreigners alone or jointly with Indonesian nationals. A minimum of two persons is required.

The services of an Indonesian Notary Public are required to organize a P.T. The deed must be in the Indonesian language and must use a name for the P.T. that the Ministry will approve. In addition, it must state its capitalization in rupiah. The capital structure must be shown in the initial Deed of Establishment, and certain percentages of the authorized capital must have been subscribed and paid in by the time the deed is approved.

The limited liability of shareholders is recognized. Shares may be in bearer or in registered form, but in practice, all shares held by foreign investors are required to be in registered form. Both common and preferred shares are permitted.

Sole traders and partnerships. The Industry Ministry's Decree No. 295/1982 rules that a sole agency agreement between an Indonesian company and foreign principal/license or patent owner can be implemented only after obtaining a letter of recognition from the Industry Ministry, and can be terminated only with prior approval from both contracting parties.

The decree stipulates that a sole agency agreement can only be terminated prior to its expiration by mutual agreement or if the sole agent is dissolved or goes bankrupt. A foreign principal can unilaterally terminate its sole agency contract with an Indonesian company due to "nonperformance" or engaging in "extremely inappropriate" activities.

A foreign principal unilaterally terminating its agreement is required to compensate the sole agent for costs incurred in marketing/distribution of the franchised goods. The amount of compensation is based on inventory of stocks, building, and plant facilities provided by the sole agent. If the foreign principal does not enter into a new sole agency contract, it must supply its old sole agent with spare parts for at least two years to assure reasonable after sales service to local buyers.

A sole agency agreement is valid for at least three years and is extendable. If assembly and manufacture is involved in the contract, terms are a minimum of five years. Only one sole agent can be appointed for the whole country by the foreign principal, but an Indonesian company can enter into several sole agency agreements. The foreign principal must provide technical assistance to its sole agent on good after-sales service practices and technical developments in the product. A foreign principal having a sole agent in Indonesia cannot make direct sales to the country, unless the agent is compensated by overriding commission.

Sole agency regulations have been a sore point in U.S. trade relations with Indonesia. They are constituted to provide full protection to Indonesian companies, but expose American and other foreign companies to a broad range of liabilities should the supplier wish to change agents. "Agent hopping" may have motivated the Indonesian government to issue the regulations, but the record of problems incurred by principals legitimately wishing to change agents has not been encouraging.

American companies attempting to sell products coming under the purview of sole agency rules would be well advised to get advice on how to secure a modicum of protection. Information can be obtained from AMCHAM in Jakarta, the American Indonesian Chamber of Commerce in New York, or the Foreign Commercial Service at the American Embassy, Jakarta. It is possible to reduce liability by having the agreement stipulate sales quotas or other performance requirements.

Representative offices. Foreign companies may open and maintain a local representative office subject to permission of the Indonesian Department of Trade and Cooperatives. The representative may be an Indonesian national or company, or a foreign national, but only one representative office per firm is permitted. Foreign trade representatives are not allowed to engage in direct sales but may participate in sales promotion or provide market research and technical advice.

Many foreign firms and trading companies have opened trade representative offices in Indonesia and some have expatriate representatives on their staffs. In many instances, representative offices of foreign companies have established close connections with Indonesian national importers so that the two companies can operate virtually as one. The Indonesian company acts as importer-distributor for overseas principals and the foreign company promotes the products and provides technical assistance.

A foreign company can only supply communications equipment if it is affiliated with a local organization, such as an agency, trade representative, or distributor that is at least 51% Indonesian owned. If this is impossible, a liaison officer who monitors projects and bids for tenders is acceptable.

Agents and distributors. The services of an aggressive, active agent have always been the most effective means of expanding sales in Indonesia. A foreign firm selling to government agencies would do well to appoint an Indonesian firm as its agent.

The import of certain types of equipment, including road rollers, hoisting and lifting apparatus, tractors, and cement-mixing machines, have to be handled by a national franchise holder or sole agent. Sole agency relationships are also required for motorcycles, cars, and trucks. An additional 126 items were added to this list from 1982 to 1986.

At the end of 1980, to spur the development of indigenous business, particularly among the "economically weak group," the government began requiring the state oil company and other government agencies to deal through Indonesian agents when purchasing imported goods and services. The government also began putting pressure on agents to deal directly with foreign manufacturers rather than third-country middle agents.

Indonesian importers traditionally have not specialized in particular product lines. Although it is advisable to set up agency arrangements with firms that handle a complementary range of products, this is not essential since substantial sales can often be made by firms active in different commodity fields. An increasing number of firms identifying themselves as suppliers of "technical goods" concentrate on general industrial machinery and equipment and have engineers on their staffs prepared to provide engineering assistance and after-sales technical support.

INVESTMENT CLIMATE

Privatization, Investment Protection, and Dispute Settlement

The Indonesian government initiated an effort in the mid-1980s to reduce regulatory obstacles to the economy. It was designed largely to stimulate growth in the non-oil sector.

In the summer of 1989, the government announced that foreign portfolio investors could purchase up to 49% of the shares in all companies (with exception of banks) listed on the Indonesian Stock Exchange. In October 1989, the government announced refinements to the 1988 financial sector deregulation packages in the areas of taxation, the stock market, and foreign banks.

As deregulation has continued, especially with the May 28, 1990 package, applications for government approval of foreign investment projects have soared. The textile and footwear industries were popular sectors for foreign investment.

Joint Ventures and Wholly Owned Subsidiaries

Under the government's deregulation program of 1986 to 1989, joint ventures with majority Indonesian ownership are now treated as domestic entities. This enables the joint venture company to distribute its own products locally, borrow from the local money market, and invest in sectors open only to domestic companies. Joint ventures are permitted to export their own products as well as goods produced by other companies.

Taxation and Regulatory Conditions

In 1985, the government simplified the personal and corporate tax laws. A U.S.-Indonesian bilateral tax treaty was ratified by the Indonesian parliament in 1988, but still awaits ratification by the U.S. Senate. Under the agreement, Indonesians in the U.S. and Americans in Indonesia would be exempted from double taxation. The delay in Senate ratification stems from the snail's pace legislative process, not from Senatorial resistance.

The Indonesian government's deregulation program of 1986 to 1989 now makes it possible for any company exporting more than 65% of its output to import its material duty free and without license restrictions regardless of the availability of comparable domestic products.

Beginning April 1, 1984, the Indonesian government placed into effect a Value-Added Tax. The VAT replaced the former complicated sales tax which resulted in higher consumer prices. The VAT rate is 10% of the sales price or, in the case of imports, the value used for calculating import duties plus all the levies imposed by customs law. In addition, there is a tax on luxury goods, with rates ranging between 5% and 30%.

FINANCING AND CAPITAL MARKETS

Indonesia maintains an open capital account, and outflows and inflows of foreign exchange are free of government controls. In November 1989, Bank Indonesia, the country's central bank, modified procedures for carrying out its dealings in foreign exchange. Previously, the bank had announced a single daily rate for foreign exchange transactions and traded in unlimited amounts of foreign exchange at that rate in response to offers and bids.

Under the new procedures, Bank Indonesia limited the time devoted to transactions at fixed rates, but has traded more actively with individual customers, predominantly banks, at negotiated rates. The new procedures provided a more flexible instrument for managing the country's foreign exchange market.

Banking and Other Financial Institutions

The banking system has been dominated by the state commercial banks, which hold 80% of total rupiah deposits. Bank Indonesia has expanded the use of its discount window, cut the discount rate, extended the repayment period of one-time credit facilities, and doubled the percentage of deposit bases that banks can borrow using overnight interbank funds. Although commercial bank credit increased 16% in 1985, most of these funds were used to "roll over" loans to financially weak local firms. The easing of rules governing the establishment and operation of banks and savings institutions generated over 350 applications to set up new banks and 120 applications to set up branches or sub-branches in first months of 1990.

Major U.S. banks with branch offices in Indonesia are: Bankers Trust Co., Chase Manhattan Bank, Chemical Bank, Citibank, Manufacturers Hanover, and Morgan Guaranty Trust Co.

The stock market and other sources of long-term capital in Indonesia remain relatively undeveloped. However, in June 1989, a second stock exchange was opened in Surabaya, beginning over-the-counter market operations.

To compensate for reductions in Indonesian government subsidies, a few state companies have floated long-term loans. New investment regulations have encouraged the sales of foreign joint venture shares on the local stock market, but strict performance requirements and excessive costs have discouraged users.

Payment Modalities

The Currency

As of mid-1990, expectations of a rupiah devaluation had gradually ebbed since the last major devaluation in 1986. The government's policy of allowing a slow downward drift of the rupiah helped maintain confidence in the Indonesian currency, as well as the competitiveness of Indonesian exports. The 1990 budget and balance-of-payments projection, was drawn up assuming an average annual 5% depreciation of the rupiah against the dollar.

Equity Finance and Privatization

In November 1989, the government authorized sales of equity in 52 state-owned enterprises. Public offerings could begin in 1991, although the government plans to spread out the sales over time so as not to disrupt the stock market. Sales of equity in public enterprises should lessen their dependence on government financing in the long run. Foreign investors in Batam Island (12 miles from Singapore) can now hold 100% equity in export projects for up to five years.

Tapping International Aid Institutions

Government organizations usually spend more than their budget allotments and are forced to take out loans from the World Bank. Thus, credit terms are probably the most important consideration when public end-users select a supplier. Japanese companies hold a big advantage by offering long-term credit with no interest charges for up to two years. Suppliers from other countries, including the United States, do not provide grace periods during which interest rates are suspended, and usually charge higher interest rates.

LICENSING, PATENTS, AND TRADEMARKS

Licensing Policy, Procedures, and Payments

In 1987 and 1988, licensing and government purchasing processes were simplified. The government announced a massive deregulation package on May 28, 1990 simplifying licensing procedures and regulations for the pharmaceutical industry and opening the market for new factories.

Under the government's deregulation program of 1986 to 1989, the number of licenses required to operate a business was reduced from four to two. In addition, companies can expand production capacity up to 30% without obtaining prior permission.

Trademark, Patent, and Copyright Protection

Trademark registrations are granted under the Trade Name and Trademarks Act (No. 21 of 1961) for 10 years from the date of registration and may be extended for like periods. The first user of a mark for a class of goods is entitled to the trademark registration for that class. In the absence of proof to the contrary, the first applicant for registration is considered to be the first to make use of the mark, provided he uses the mark within six months after the registration for the covered goods.

There is no provision for opposition before the trademark office under Indonesian law. However, once a mark is registered, a party who believes the registration violates his rights may file a petition to cancel the registration with the District Court of Jakarta. The petition must be filed within nine months of publication of the registration. However, it has become more difficult to obtain favorable judgements from the courts.

The government is now considering possible revisions of its trademark law to make it more compatible with international practices. In 1989, the United States and Indonesian governments implemented a bilateral copyright agreement extending copyright protection to American firms and individuals in the Indonesian market.

The Indonesian parliament passed the country's first patent bill in October 1989. It was signed into law by President Soeharto in November 1989 and took effect on August 1, 1991. Its provisions largely follow those of the World Intellectual Property Organization (WIPO) model for developing countries. It provides product protection *inter alia* for chemical and pharmaceutical products.

The copyright law in force in Indonesia is Act No. 6 of April 12, 1982. Foreign works are not eligible for protection unless they are first published in Indonesia.

Effectiveness of Legal Safeguards

The enforcement of copyright protection for published materials, particularly translations of foreign books, video tapes, and cassette tapes has been lax. The 1989 copyright agreement between the United States and Indonesia has not been totally enforced, particularly in the areas of computer software and motion pictures. On the whole, intellectual property protection in Indonesia has improved greatly over the past few years.

VISITING AND LOCATING

General Travel Checklist

Visas

A visa is required for a visit to Indonesia of any duration, although business people from Indonesia's ASEAN partners and 23 other countries, including the United States, may obtain free visas on arrival.

The granting of free visas to business people at ports of entry is limited to visits for purposes of investigating investment and trade opportunities, or discussions between a foreign company and its local office or partners. Those obtaining visas upon arrival are not permitted to conclude commercial transactions, engage in local employment, or perform professional or technical services. Persons traveling to Indonesia for these purposes or other business purposes not specified here should apply for regular business visas at an Indonesian embassy or consulate. Regular business visas are issued for visits up to five weeks and can be extended for an additional six months.

Temporary resident visas are valid for six months to one year and are issued exclusively to experts required for national development and to expatriates who are involved in training or other educational or scientific programs in line with prevailing government regulations. Dependents can also qualify for those visas.

Currency

The currency in Indonesia is the rupiah, a managed float tied to a basket of currencies from Indonesia's major trading partners. There are virtually no exchange restrictions.

Getting Around

The internal transport network of Indonesia is most developed on Java and the northern and southern parts of Sumatra, Madura, and Bali. It is relatively undeveloped on Kalimantan, Sulawesi, and Irian Jaya. Most cities on Java, Sumatra, Sulawesi, and Bali are connected by highway and secondary roads.

There are railways on Java, Madura, and Sumatra, with total track mileage of approximately 3,900 miles, of which 3,000 miles are on Java. The railways are used intensively for both freight transportation and passenger services.

Accommodations and Housing

Hotels in Indonesia are not expensive but include air conditioning, swimming pools, restaurants, shopping, secretarial services, translation facilities, and telex. Hotel development is booming; as many as 30,000 additional rooms will be available by 1993.

Electricity Supply

In the past, the electrical current was 110V 50c. Most areas are rapidly changing over to 220/50. Some houses may have both 110 and 220 volt supplies. There are frequent power brown-outs, and it is suggested that each home has its own stand-by generator. Foreign residents usually use air conditioners.

Ports, hospitals, airports, radio and television stations, movie houses, and hotels all have their own electricity-generating equipment for standby purposes, and, in some cases, to meet their own operating power needs.

Telecom, Postal, and Courier Services

As of 1989, Indonesia's telephone density was one of the lowest in the world: 0.51 phones per 100 population. There were 5,104 public pay phones. International connections can be made through INTELSAT and submarine cable networks. In 1989, 132 countries could be directly dialed from 19 Indonesian cities.

Indonesia has two domestic telecommunications satellites, supported by over 300 ground stations. Indonesia has a cellular telephone system, introduced in 1986, with equipment supplied by Ericsson. The first phase of the cellular network has eight radio base stations and 18 cells that cover Jakarta and Bandung. Phase one capacity is 10,000 subscribers. Cellular radio services are very expensive; the installation of car radio sets costs about U.S. $6,300 and connection time is also very expensive.

The current Five-Year Plan (1989-1994) includes the following projects in the telecommunications field:

- Installation of an additional 1.4 million telephone lines, 15,200 telex lines and expansion of gentex, and 71,000 public pay phones.

- Expansions of terrestrial long distance facilities; expansions of international direct dialing to achieve access to 157 countries from 40 cities in Indonesia.

- Expansion of other services such as radio paging, Birofax, and data communications.

Business Hours

Business hours are flexible depending on the business and the location. The following schedule can provide a good general guideline:

Commerce:	8:00 a.m. to 3:00 p.m. Monday through Thursday
	8:00 a.m. to 11:30 a.m. Friday
	8:00 a.m. to 2:00 p.m. Saturday
Banks:	8:00 a.m. to 12:00 p.m. Monday through Friday
	8:00 a.m. to 11:00 a.m. Saturday
Shops:	9:00 a.m. to 6:00 p.m. (or later) Monday through Friday
Government:	8:00 a.m. to 3:00 p.m. Monday through Thursday
	8:00 a.m. to 11:30 a.m. Friday
	8:00 a.m. to 2:00 p.m. Saturday

Indonesia takes 13 holidays per year. Some are fixed date holidays, and others vary with the lunar calendar.

What to Wear

Indonesia straddles the equator, which means that both temperatures and humidity tend to be uncomfortably high by U.S. standards. Fortunately, dress codes are informal. Use of a jacket with tie is sufficient for men during working hours. Lightweight cottons are worn year round, with two changes a day frequently required. Synthetics are uncomfortable in hot and humid weather. For men, a long sleeve batik shirt is considered formal wear. The American Women's Association publication, "Introducing Indonesia," lists the names and addresses of stores and shops where men's, women's, and children's wear can be purchased.

Health Care

Indonesian authorities require persons arriving in Indonesia from yellow fever-infected areas to possess an international certificate of vaccination against yellow fever. In addition, it is recommended that preventive measures against malaria be taken if traveling outside of Jakarta or other major Indonesian cities.

The general level of community sanitation and public health awareness is low throughout Indonesia. Local hazards include typhoid, hepatitis, cholera, amoebiasis, enteric parasites, tuberculosis, and common infections. Cholera, typhoid, paratyphoid, and tetanus vaccinations are strongly recommended for persons remaining in Indonesia for an extended period.

Medication for stomach or intestinal ailments should be included in a traveling kit. Except for large hotels in Bali, tap water is considered unsafe to drink.

The Media

Indonesia's national television station, TVRI, began in 1962. Only since 1976, when the PALAPA satellite system began, could TVRI's broadcasts be seen by all Indonesians with television sets.

Sightseeing and Tourist Information

Indonesia is stepping up efforts to expand its tourist industry. Temples, parks, and historic buildings are being spruced up. Government-sponsored tourism exhibitions are making the rounds in the United States.

The Short-Term Business Visitor

Airlines Serving

Indonesia's flag-carrier airline, Garuda Indonesian Airways, is government-owned. All provincial capitals are accessible by air.

Immigration and Work Permits

A person who wishes to continue employment in Indonesia must be in possession of a work permit. It should be noted that foreigners may be employed in Indonesia only in occupations which cannot be filled by Indonesian nationals. Foreigners are barred from practicing law, and restrictions apply in certain service sectors, such as accounting and certain types of insurance.

However, there is normally no difficulty in obtaining permission for employment of expatriate managers and technicians where the Indonesian government believes qualified Indonesians are not available to fill the positions. The government issues a list of professions in every sector of business open to the employment of expatriate personnel and of the working period permitted.

Foreign and domestic investors must submit a manpower employment plan to BKPM with a copy to the Minister of Manpower to obtain approval for expatriate employee work permits.

The Labor Force

Employment and labor relations. A major constraint on the private sector is the scarcity of certain categories of skilled labor, particularly mid-level technicians, certain types of engineers, accountants, managers, and supervisors. The situation became acute in the rapidly growing banking sector during 1989; new banking units bid away experienced staff from older banks, and salaries in this sector soared.

Rising official concern about the development of Indonesian management is reflected in regulations requiring greater numbers of Indonesians in supervisory and managerial positions, even though qualified Indonesians in both areas are in short supply. The government expects foreign investors to train and develop Indonesian nationals to replace expatriates within a reasonable period of time.

Training. A large gap exists between the demand for university graduates with technical degrees and the outputs of local universities or polytechnic institutes.

INDONESIA

KEY CONTACTS

American Embassy Contacts

American Embassy Jakarta
Medan Merdeka Selatan 5
APO San Francisco 96356
    Tel: 62/21-360-360
    Telex: 44218 AMEMB JKT

Ambassador:	John C. Monjo
Deputy Chief of Mission:	Michael V. Connors
Political Section:	Timothy M. Carney
Economic Section:	Bruce F. Duncombe
Commercial Section:	Paul T. Walters
Labor Officer:	Gail P. Scott
Administrative Section:	David A. Roberts
Regional Security Officer:	William A. Cole
Agricultural Section:	Kenneth L. Murray
Public Affairs Officer:	Michael Yaki
Office of the Defense Attache:	Col. John D. Mussells, U.S.A.

Business Contacts

American Indonesian Chamber of Commerce
Wayne J. Forrest, Executive Director
711 Third Avenue
17th Floor
New York, NY 10017
    Tel: 212/687-4505
    Fax: 212/867-9882

Resources Management International Inc.
Walt Flinn, Director
2000 L Street, NW #200
Washington, DC 20036
    Tel: 202/223-1020
    FAX: 202/775-5199
    Telex: 47129 RMIJKT

Consulate General of the Republic of Indonesia

Head Office:
5 East 68th Street
New York, NY 10021
   Tel: 212/879-0600

Houston:
190 Post Oak Boulevard #1900
Three Post Oak Central
Houston, TX 77056
   Tel: 713/626-3291

Chicago:
2 Illinois Center #1422
233 N. Michigan
Chicago, IL 60601
   Tel: 312/938-0707

Los Angeles:
645 South Mariposa Avenue
Los Angeles, CA 90005
   Tel: 213/383-5126

San Francisco:
111 Columbus Avenue
San Francisco, CA 94133
   Tel: 415/474-9571

Key Contacts in the Public and Private Sector

Government and Quasi-Governmental

Minister of Communications: Cicilio Sukarman.

Advocates improved telecommunications network and especially encourages American involvement.

Minister of Trade: Dr. Arifin M. Siregar.

Junior Minister of Trade: Dr. J. Soedradjat Djiwandono

Minister of Tourism Posts and Telecommunications: Soesilo Soedarman

Chairman of BKPM, Investment Coordinating Board: Sanyoto Sastrowardoyo

Chamber of Commerce

American Chamber of Commerce in Indonesia (AMCHAM)
Citibank Building, 8th floor,
Jl. M.H. Thamrin 55, Jakarta.
Tel: 332602. Telex: 44368 CITIBANK IA.

Affiliated with the Asia-Pacific Council of American Chambers of Commerce (AP-CAC). Its membership of 400 (as of May 1986) consists of leading U.S. firms with offices in Indonesia and additional associates, individuals, and special members. The chamber has prepared a number of useful guides to doing business in Indonesia, including an annual country paper. It also assists U.S. firms that are assessing business opportunities by staging AMCHAM briefing breakfasts at the requestor's expense.

American-Indonesian Chamber of Commerce
711 Third Ave.
New York, NY 10017
Tel: (212) 687-4505
Executive Director: Wayne J. Forrest.

Founded in 1949, it now represents 120 American companies, multinational corporations, and Indonesian companies. It has an active program of monthly lunches featuring speakers knowledgeable on Indonesia and briefing programs for newly-appointed Indonesian and American government officials. The chamber also publishes "Outlook/Indonesia," a quarterly publication containing interpretations of new Indonesian policies, sectorial reviews, summaries of recent chamber activities, and an executive secretary's column.

Board of Trade/World Trade Center

United States-Indonesia Trade Investment Council (USITIC)
Chairman of the Executive Committee: Walter Flynn

Founded in 1985, initiated by then Indonesian Ambassador to the United States, Soesilo Soedarman, now Minister of Posts, Telecommunications, and Tourism. Objectives are to encourage U.S. companies to invest in Indonesia by forming joint ventures and to identify (for the government of Indonesia) those restraints that discouraged U.S. investors.

Professional and Trade Associations

Indonesian Chamber of Commerce and Industry (KADIN)
Jl. Merdeka Timur II, Jakarta

The major trade association in Indonesia whose membership includes representatives from private industry, as well as cooperatives, utilities, public corporations, and state-owned enterprises throughout Indonesia.

In addition to associations of a general nature, there are numerous enterprises with homogenous interests in trade, industry, transportation, or other sectors of the economy that have organized specialized or professional associations. These can be found in the publication, "Standard Trade and Industry Directory for Indonesia," which may be requested from the Indonesian Embassy, Washington, Commercial Section.

Associations of importers and exporters, most of which are organized on a commodity basis, are also members of an umbrella organization, the Importers Association of Indonesia (GINSI), Jl. Majapahit 1, Jakarta, and the Indonesian Association of Exporters (GPEI), Jl. Kramat Rava Nos. 4 and 6.

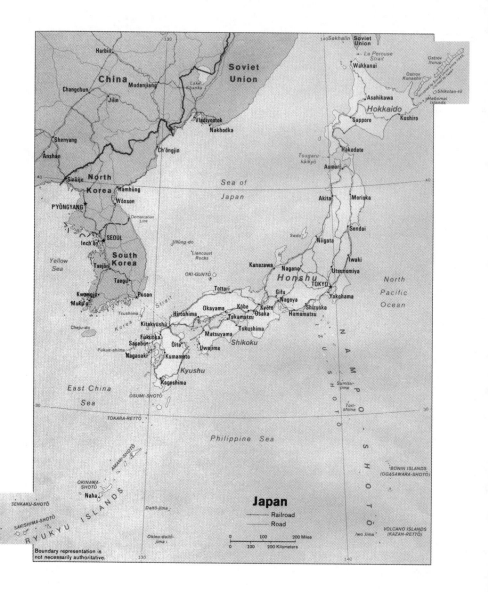

Japan

Railroad
Road

0   100   200 Miles
0   100   200 Kilometers

Boundary representation is
not necessarily authoritative.

JAPAN

JAPAN

In a Nutshell

		Urban Population
Population (1992)	123,800,000	76.9%

Main Urban Areas		Percentage of Total
Tokyo	8,163,000	6.5
Yokohama	3,220,000	2.3
Osaka	2,624,000	2.1
Kobe	1,477,000	1.1
Kyoto	1,461,000	1.1
Kawasaki	1,174,000	0.9

Land Area   145,874 square miles
377,815 square kilometers

Comparable European State   Slightly larger than Finland
Comparable U.S. State   Slightly smaller than California

Language   Japanese
Common Business Language   English
Currency   Yen (1Y = 100 sen)

Best Air Connection

New York-Tokyo (daily)
Chicago-Tokyo (daily)
Washington, DC-Tokyo (Tues., Thurs., Sat.)
San Francisco-Tokyo (daily)
Los Angeles-Tokyo (daily)
Japan Air Lines 800/525-3663

Los Angeles-Tokyo (daily)
New York-Tokyo (Mon., Tues., Thurs., Fri., Sat.)
Washington, DC-Tokyo (daily except Thurs.)
All Nippon Airlines 800/235-9262

Best Hotel   Century Hyatt ($342/night as of 2/92)

CHAPTER CONTENTS

INTRODUCTION AND REGIONAL ORIENTATION

Geographical and Historical Background

Japan's dense population (currently at approximately 125 million), geographical isolation, and poor endowment of natural resources have contributed significantly to the country's reliance on external trade. Despite periodic trade surpluses since its postwar recovery, Japan's major imbalances are a phenomena of the past decade. However, the Japanese Ministry of Finance reported the fourth consecutive annual decline in the nation's trade surplus to $52.4 billion for 1990.

The Japanese economy experienced its first postwar recession — as defined by the American standard of two consecutive quarters of economic contraction — after the first of the 1970 oil shocks. Although growth slowed in early 1991, the Japanese economy remains healthy with a 3.5% GNP expansion. The current slowdown is largely attributable to the Bank of Japan's tight monetary policy to combat inflation, running at about 4.5% at the start of 1991. The relatively high 8% long-term prime rate in January 1991 was expected to curtail the high capital spending growth of 17% for three consecutive years, and thus sustain the slowdown.

Japan's inflation and declining trade surpluses indicate that the economy is changing from an export-driven economy to a U.S.-desired economy based on domestic demand. Not only has the overall trade surplus declined 18.5% from 1989 and 37% from its high in 1987, but exports to the United States fell for the first time in eight years. Moreover, the mild inflation of 1991 is attributable to heavy consumer and business spending in 1989 and 1990.

Japan continues to combat spiraling real estate prices. Not only are Tokyo land prices 100 to 125 times the cost of comparable real estate in the United States, but prices are escalating at an annual rate of about 35%.

Consumer Demand

The increase in domestic demand reflects consumers' responses to long-term fiscal and monetary policy, demonstrating significant sociologically-based consumer behavior changes in Japan. Among these changes is the proliferation of the "akirame rich," young and middle-aged Japanese who have abandoned the prospect of home-ownership due to the exorbitant real estate prices. The mortgageless akirame rich have considerable disposable income that goes largely toward consumption.

As the Japanese traveled, exposing themselves to different cultures and economies, they became increasingly vocal about high domestic prices and willing to use the appreciated value of the yen to purchase imports they perceive as reliable.

Consequently, Japan's industrial base has changed to keep pace with domestic demand and competitive pressures from imports.

Despite Japan's traditional emphasis on homogeneity and "the group," consumers recently demanded more attention to individuality, leading to the segmentation of markets. Segmentation revealed niches such as "the silver society" of retired people and children with ready cash from traditional Japanese holiday gift giving.

Consumer consciousness resulted in numerous marketing innovations, including: roadside discounters, do-it-yourself home centers, catalog and mail order sales, and specialty stores. The shifting lifestyles and increased leisure activities of Japanese society in general and the country's youth in particular facilitated this growth.

Brand consciousness and increased desire for individuality have caused a greater emphasis on product appearance and its packaging as status symbols. This trend provides numerous opportunities for exporting to and investing in Japan.

Political/Institutional Infrastructure

Japan is governed by a parliamentary democracy, dominated by the Liberal Democratic party (LDP). Despite a series of scandals in the late 1980s, the LDP rebounded under the leadership of current Prime Minister Toshiki Kaifu, reestablishing its hold on local government throughout Japan.

The government bureaucracy or cabinet is another key player in policy formulation, drafting proposals which are later sent through the LDP system and then to the Diet, the Japanese parliament. Unlike the U.S. government, over 80% of the bills proposed in Japan are initiated by the cabinet, which enjoys a 75% success rate.

After leaving the cabinet, a proposal goes to the LDP for consideration by the respective subcommittee of the LDP's Policy Affairs Research Committee (PARC). Each of the PARC subcommittees interfaces with a counterpart in the bureaucracy to ensure harmonious policy formulation and coordination of objectives. After leaving the PARC, a proposal remains within the LDP and is now considered by the party's Executive Council. Approval here is ipso facto party authorization.

The proposal is finally considered by the Diet. The Diet consists of two houses: the House of Representatives (the lower house) and the House of Councillors (the upper house). In practice, the lower house is much more powerful than the upper house, both of which are controlled by the LDP. The Diet wields relatively little power in policy formulation because at this stage other LDP party members in the bureaucracy and at party headquarters have already determined the thrust of the proposal. Opposition parties, such as the labor supported Japan Socialist party can force concessions from the LDP by using their 25% proposal-blockage rate as leverage.

The last major political player is big business, affecting both the bureaucracy and parties through substantial corporate giving. Especially important is the Keidanren (Federation of Economic Organizations), which represents about 100 major trade associations and 750 large corporations.

Trade Flows

Despite massive trade surpluses with its trading partners over the past ten years, Japan has made significant progress in changing these imbalances. As mentioned previously, Japan's present trade surplus is $52.4 billion, marking the fourth straight annual decline in this figure and a far cry from the $86.4 billion high-water mark in 1987.

The major contributor to the large imbalances is Japan's largest trading partner, the United States, with a $49 billion account deficit in 1989. Other major contributors include South Korea, Germany, and Taiwan. The United States takes approximately 35% of Japan's exports while supplying about 23% of Japan's imports. The People's Republic of China is Japan's second largest trading partner, followed by Saudi Arabia and Indonesia. In an effort to improve strained United States-Japan trade relations and create a friendlier means of settling trade disputes, both countries are participating in the Structural Impediments Initiative (SII).

The United States claims that its trade deficits vis-a-vis Japan are due to a number of factors, including the following:

1. The United States claims that Japan must do more at a faster pace to open its markets, especially in retail, by simplifying it distribution system.

2. Japan is accused of exclusionary business practices, such as the dango system, which collusively awards bids on a rotating system among Japanese vendors.

3. The United States claims that Japan must lower its extremely high savings rate in order to encourage personal consumption.

POLICIES TO ATTRACT NEW BUSINESSES

In an effort to increase imports, the Japanese Ministry of International Trade and Industry (MITI) initiated an import expansion program in early 1990. A key element in the program is the abolition of customs duties for approximately 1,000 items, including computers, semiconductors, telecommunications equipment, and almost all machinery. The government will institute a duty drawback system for items imported to Japan and later exported.

Also, the program established a tax system promoting the importation of manufactured goods. Under the system, manufacturers that have increased imports of authorized products by over 10% are granted a tax credit equal to 5% of the increase, or they may take 10% extra depreciation (20% for machinery).

The program also promotes imports through the establishment of a "Grass-Roots Internationalization Center" and an "International Distribution Center." The former creates a database and installs the hardware needed to support the database throughout Japan. The database will carry information on foreign products held by the Japan External Trade Organization (JETRO). Terminals will also be installed in the JETRO offices of major trading partners to facilitate exporting to Japan.

Foreign exporters can take advantage of $1.6 billion in low-interest loans from the Export-Import Bank of Japan. Of course, eligible Japanese firms are also competing for these funds. Four other major public financing corporations offer loans to domestic firms for import expansion: the Japan Development Bank, the Small Business Finance Corporation, the People's Finance Corporation and the Japan Small Business Corporation.

APPROACHING THE MARKET

Trade and Investment Decision-Making Infrastructure

The key bureaucratic entities in the trade and investment policy formulation arena are the Ministry of International Trade and Industry (MITI), the Ministry of Finance, and the Economic Planning Agency (EPA). Also, the nation's central bank, the Bank of Japan, exercises considerable control over foreign investment and, to a lesser extent, external trade.

MITI is charged with policy-formulation and negotiation of international trade agreements and is responsible for implementation and enforcement of policy. The Ministry of Finance handles matters that require an allocation of funds and those involving taxation. Thus, there is often an overlap in jurisdiction, which has in the past led to interministerial squabbling. The Economic Planning Agency is under control of the Prime Minister and is his vehicle for achieving trade and investment goals.

The Bank of Japan has far more control over international trade and investment than does its U.S. counterpart. For example, a foreign investor intending to acquire stock in its Japanese subsidiary must file a notification with the Bank of Japan. Although such notifications are almost automatically approved, the Bank of Japan does have the power to disapprove such action. Similar notifications must be given to the ministry of the industry concerned.

Pertinent trade and investment laws include the Foreign Exchange Law, the Anti-Monopoly Law, the Commercial Law, and the Tax Law.

Consulting/Legal Services

Japanese Government

There are a number of good state consulting services available. In the United States, MITI's affiliate is the Japan External Trade Organization (JETRO). JETRO provides assistance for foreign firms considering investment in and trade with Japan. Despite what may appear to be admirable intentions, JETRO is notoriously unresponsive and aloof. Some speculate that the organization is simply a ploy by MITI devised to reduce trade friction.

The Manufactured Imports Promotion Organization (MIPRO) of Japan is a MITI affiliate seeking to expand Japan's manufactured imports. The U.S. address of MIPRO is 2000 L Street, NW, Suite 616, Washington, DC 20036 (tel: 202/659-3729).

U.S. Government

The U.S. Department of Commerce's International Trade Administration (ITA) has export and investment consulting services available both in the United States and in Japan. (For information about these services call the Department of Commerce at 202/377-2425.) Specific services include the following:

- Agent/distributor service
- World traders data reports
- Trade opportunities program
- Export mailing lists
- Country market surveys

The Export Development Office (EDO) in Tokyo works with the ITA on exhibitions, trade missions, trade fairs, and assists individual U.S. business people. The EDO address is as follows: World Import Mart, 7th Floor, 1-3 Higashi Ikebukuro 3 chome, Toshima-ku, Tokyo 107 (tel: 03-987-2441).

In addition, the Commercial Section of the U.S. Embassy provides counseling and assistance to U.S. businesses. Contact them in Tokyo at 03-583-7141.

For questions regarding legal issues, contact the State Department Legal and Judicial Affairs, East Asia Branch at 202/647-3675. For information on export licenses contact the U.S. Department of Commerce's Export Administration at 202/377-2752.

The American Chamber of Commerce in Japan (ACCJ) offers advice in various trade areas. Contact them at the following address and phone number: Fukide No.2 Bldg., 1-21, Toranomon 4-chome, Minato-ku, Tokyo 105.

Private Firms

The three top public relations/consulting firms that have experience with foreign companies are Burson-Marsteller Dentsu; Gavin and Anderson; and Hill and Knowlton.

Agents/Distributors and Trading Companies

The selection of the agent/distributor is a critical step and should proceed from a comprehensive analysis of the market, a firm's marketing strategy, and individual agent/distributor competence. Undoubtedly, the complex distribution system in Japan requires close and patient examination. Distribution troubles such as redundancy and inefficiency in the marketing channel may be the difference between price competitiveness and stagnant sales.

It is important to note that in Japan, products come to the end-user through several wholesalers and a retailer. Wholesalers can be categorized depending on their location, stage in distribution, and product inventory. For example, a "direct" wholesaler buys from the manufacturer and sells directly to a retailer, whereas an "ordinary" wholesaler buys the product only to pass it on to other wholesalers. More complicated yet, an "intermediate" wholesaler will both buy from and sell to other wholesalers. Obviously, channels will vary according to the specific industry in question.

Another wholesaler classification is the "tonya," which depending on their functions are either limited or general wholesalers. The general wholesaler fulfills the three main wholesaling functions: trading, distributing goods, and distributing information. Limited wholesalers, on the other hand, will perform only one or two of these functions. Again, the type needed depends on the industry specifics and the firm's marketing plan.

Although methods of importing abound in the Japanese business environment, the most prevalent is the use of trading companies. Although some "tonya" carry on trading functions, if circumstances permit, it may be preferable to employ a single import agent, consolidating the sales, promotion, and miscellaneous functions. U.S. trade negotiators, legislators, and business people consistently harp on the multilayered and complex distribution system as the most glaring barrier to the Japanese market. Japan has roughly the same number of wholesalers to support a population that is about half that of the United States.

The great number of retail outlets stems from consumers' low mobility in congested urban areas, lack of shelf space due to smaller stores and exorbitant real estate, and Japanese penchant for fresh foods (such as fish). In order to make the numerous small-lot deliveries, the wholesale side has had to keep pace with the size and structure of the retail system.

Moreover, since the mom-and-pop stores depend on their suppliers for credit, a multitiered wholesaling system has emerged as a means of spreading the risk of retail default. Finally, the Japanese emphasis on after-sales service has engendered a consignment inventory system which leads back to the manufacturer. Thus, the multitiered distribution system has developed to support the flow of goods back through the channel.

Obviously, the creation of a distribution plan is a painstaking effort, but distribution is probably the most common pitfall of foreign entities doing business in Japan. The aforementioned government agencies and/or consulting firms should be employed in selecting marketing channels and choosing agents/distributors and trading companies.

Re-Export

Another outlet for goods manufactured in Japan is re-exportation. Products assembled in Japan and re-exported are eligible for tariff refunds under MITI's "duty drawback" system. The drawback system opens the door to the option of re-exporting to Southeast Asia or elsewhere in the world.

Setting Up Offices in Japan

Although real estate prices are very high throughout Japan, the cases are extreme in Tokyo. Consequently, the Japanese government has introduced tax and zoning laws to more evenly distribute the population across the nation. The safest procedure in finding the appropriate space is negotiating with a real estate agent that specializes in foreign affiliates. An English speaking agent will be well worth the additional amount paid for this "specialty."

Monthly rent in prime Tokyo space ranges from 80,000 to 90,000 yen per 3.3 square meters. Rent for small to mid-sized buildings in central Tokyo runs from

30,000 to 40,000 yen per 3.3 square meters. Hence, the manager must plan for efficiency to minimize the space rented. One option is establishing another office with less critical location operations in a less expensive area, even outside of Tokyo if circumstances permit.

The main costs include key money (a deposit), a brokerage fee to the real estate agent, and rent itself. Key money will run about one million yen per 3.3 square meters in a good building, although this amount is refunded at the end of the lease, normally two years.

In hiring employees, linguistic ability should not be a big factor in the decision. Except for employees dealing with upper-level management and secretaries of directors, more emphasis should be placed on competence and other nonlinguistic skills.

In 1990, the annual salary of a director of a major Japanese firm was approximately 20 million yen and the average for a president of such a firm was 40 to 50 million yen. A non-English speaking section chief commanded an annual salary of about 15 million yen. A secretary speaking fluent English earned between three to four million yen.

Telephone service takes approximately one week to install and costs approximately 80,000 yen, including the installation charge. Exchanging a business card or meishi is crucial in Japan and customary when meeting for the first time. One hundred cards (with Japanese print on the front and English on the back) costs 5,000 to 10,000 yen.

Interpreting (oral) costs about 30,000 yen for a half day or 50,000 yen for a full day. Translation (written) from English to Japanese is about 2,000 yen per page. A Japanese to English translation costs about double, and technical translation or interpretation costs about three times as much.

Corporate taxes are somewhat higher than in other leading countries. About half of ordinary profit has to be paid as corporate tax, although this varies with the unique status of each company. Employees pay income tax and local tax.

Depending on the nature of your business, you may wish to establish a representative office before starting a branch office or a subsidiary. Representative offices need not be registered at the District Legal Affairs Bureau and are not subject to corporate taxation.

No permits or approvals are necessary, except for firms involved in banking, securities, or insurance. A representative office must refrain from commercial transactions and limit its activities to advertising, conducting market research, or basic research, and in certain instances purchasing assets.

INVESTMENT CLIMATE

Dispute Settlement

Japan's legal system is somewhat slower than its U.S. counterpart. Consequently, businesses are more inclined to settle differences out of court. Should an out-of-court settlement fail, however, Japan offers equitable due process.

Subsidiary Versus Branch Office

Although establishing a branch office is less time-consuming and less expensive than starting a subsidiary, the latter offers numerous advantages. It is perceived as more permanent and is in a much stronger borrowing, leasing, and sales position. Moreover, the subsidiary reduces the parent company's (and any other investors') liability to the extent of investment. Also, there are no net Japanese tax advantages to establishing a branch. However, the branch formation may be preferable for U.S. taxation purposes if the Japanese entity is expected to sustain losses over a considerable period of time.

As a subsidiary or a joint venture (discussed later), the operation forms a Kabushiki Kaisha (KK), the equivalent of a U.S. corporation, in which ownership and management are separate. The initial capital structure must have at least one-quarter of all authorized stock outstanding. The minimum paid-in capital is 400,000 yen at formation and the minimum number of investors is eight, seven of which must be resident "promoters" and one "subscriber," the U.S. parent. The minimum paid-in value of 400,000 yen is based on a minimum share price of 50,000 for each of the eight original investors. For tax purposes, the Japanese KK usually has a significantly greater debt-to-equity ratio than its U.S. counterpart.

The capitalization plan requires filing with the Ministry of Finance and is controlled by the Foreign Exchange Law. Notification of requests for equity investment are also given to the Bank of Japan, which almost automatically approves the request. A two-week waiting period applies in certain industries. Notification of requests for debt financing is also filed with the Bank of Japan and is normally approved very quickly. The KK must register with the corporate registry office in the district of the company's headquarters within two weeks of the inaugural meetings of the directors and shareholders.

Joint Ventures

Foreign investors establishing joint ventures are required to notify the Ministry of Finance and the ministry governing that industry through the Bank of Japan. These filings are in accordance with the Foreign Exchange Law. According to the Anti-Monopoly Law, filings must also be made with the Fair Trade Commission within three months of the agreement's execution. Many of the capital structure requirements that apply to wholly owned subsidiaries also apply to joint ventures.

Franchising

Japan is the second largest market for U.S. franchisers. Since being viewed as a distribution method circumventing traditional Japanese methods, franchising has continued expanding into different sectors of the economy. Japanese franchisers require either contract fees or royalties, rather than both, which is the U.S. practice. Although the Japanese place great importance on branding and product loyalty, U.S. franchisers have succeeded in introducing "business format franchising," offering not only trade name licensing, but transfer of management skill and a standard or formula for operations.

Corporate Taxation

Corporate taxes in Japan are higher than those in other leading industrial nations. Corporations are subject to national taxation on aggregate income from all sources. For the tax year 1990, the maximum corporate income tax rate was 37.5%. The tax rate for the first 8 million yen is 28%, provided the KK has paid-in capital of 100 million yen or less. Local governments also levy taxes. A "blue return" may be filed with the approval of the Japanese tax authorities.

FINANCING AND CAPITAL MARKETS

Financial Institutions

Liberalization of financial markets and the internationalization of the yen are other sources of trade friction between Japan and the United States/EC. However, some progress has been made in the entry of foreign operations into trust banking and partial liberalization of yen CDs. Other market-opening measures include the elimination of caps on banks' overseas lending, easing restrictions on the euroyen market for nonresidents, and the establishment of a yen denominated bankers' acceptance market.

The securities industry has made several other regulatory changes, including bolstering of the previously ignored Securities and Exchange Law governing insider trading. Persistent complaints from overseas has caused strict penalties on insider trading practices. Another recent change is the introduction of a new tax system applicable to all capital gains.

Foreign firms are now able to become members of the Tokyo Stock Exchange, the Nikkei. Currently, there are 45 foreign securities companies with branches in Japan. Half of these are Nikkei members trading stocks on their own account.

Despite the advent of these foreign firms, the market is clearly dominated by the "Big Four" brokerage houses (Nomura, Daiwa, Nikko, and Yamaichi) which enjoy a combined market share of 42.2% and have proportional profits. Contributing to these profits are fixed brokerage commissions, which place the foreign newcomers at an extreme disadvantage. Another source of conflict in this industry is the banking-affiliated securities firms, a practice prohibited in most industrial nations.

On the banking side, new international capital adequacy standards have been introduced, creating a credit crunch and depressing the stock market. Other interest rate liberalization measures will continue to force up rates and encourage greater competition. The new capital adequacy standards also put a squeeze on a bank's profits, creating a new financial futures market as a risk-hedging mechanism.

LICENSING, PATENTS, AND TRADEMARKS

Licensing

Technology transfer is governed by the Foreign Exchange Law, according to which foreign entities executing licensing contracts with Japanese nationals must give prior notice to the Ministry of Finance and any other ministry that controls the industry in question. The 30-day waiting period is normally waived and agreements can be executed on the same day that notice is tendered. Exceptions to this norm include license agreements with values of over 100,000,000 yen and specifically regulated technology transfers. Specially regulated industries include: aircraft, weapons, atomic energy, space development, computer components, innovative materials, petroleum, and leather.

In addition, licensing agreements are subject to approval by the Japan Fair Trade Commission.

Intellectual Property

Japan and the United States subscribe to the conditions of the Paris Convention for the Protection of Industrial Property. However, this does not protect an American firm from intellectual property infringement if the property right was granted in the United States only. Protection is granted on a country-by-country basis and is not yet transferable. Victims of property right violations may seek redress in the Japanese courts under the Japanese Copyright Act.

VISITING AND LOCATING

The business visitor needs both a passport and a visa to enter and work. The purpose of the visit determines the type of visa issued. Alien registration is also required if the visit exceeds 90 days. Immunization and health certificates are required for entry, and transit through immigration and quarantine is automatic, provided your passport and visa are valid.

Customs clearance is equally uncomplicated. Japan allows an oral declaration of personal effects except in three instances: arrival by ship, unaccompanied baggage, or carrying in excess of the roughly $400 duty-free allowance.

Language

While hotel, retail, and restaurant employees speak some English, fluency and comprehension are limited. Technical matters are best handled by reputable translators or interpreters. A reasonable price for a technical interpretation for a half-day is 60,000 to 90,000 yen, but only 30,000 yen for business-related interpretation. Translation from Japanese into English is 4,000 yen per single-spaced page for nontechnical matter. Similar translation from English into Japanese is 2,000 yen per page.

Currency

Japan does not restrict the amount of currency brought into the country, nor does it limit the convertibility or repatriation of funds. Major American credit cards (American Express, Visa, Master Card, Diner's Club) are usually accepted.

Measurement Standards

Japan uses the metric system. The electricity standard is 100 volts and Japanese electrical outlets will accommodate most U.S. appliances. Both 110 and 220 volt outlets are available in Japanese hotels.

Hotels and Restaurants

Although western-style hotels abound in Japan, reservations should be made as early as possible due to demand. Also, comparable accommodations are considerably higher than in the United States. Cleanliness is the norm in Japanese restaurants and water is entirely safe, not only in the restaurants but throughout the country. Although tipping is not expected, all hotel and night clubs and some restaurants include a 10% to 15% service charge in addition to a 10% tax. It is customary when entering a traditional Japanese restaurant or home to remove one's shoes in exchange for slippers while inside.

Transportation

Rail transportation in Japan is fast, prompt, and uncomplicated. Commuter train fare varies with distance and is well-connected with long-distance trains and local subway trains. Although crowded, local subway trains provide convenient and frequent service that usually ends at midnight. Subway stations and directions are marked in English and Japanese. Taxis are abundant but rather expensive. Tipping is not expected and cars are very clean.

Helpful Tips for the First-Time Visitor

- Carry a matchbook with the name and address of your hotel in Japanese so someone can help you get back if you get lost.
- Have your hotel concierge or a business contact write down the address of your next destination in Japanese.
- Avoid subways at the following commuter hours: 7:30 a.m. until 9:30 a.m. and 5:00 p.m. until 7:00 p.m.
- Remember, the trains and subways stop operating at midnight. Hang on to your subway ticket; you need it to exit at your destination.
- For your convenience, carry subway change. You will need between 120 and 260 yen to return to your starting point.
- If you can't tell which subway ticket to buy, buy the cheapest and be ready to pay the station attendant at your destination.
- In the evening, look for cabs that have red lights to indicate they are unoccupied. Green lights indicate they are occupied.
- Taxi doors only open and close on the left side; doors are operated by the driver.

Holidays

The following is a list of national holidays celebrated in Japan:

January 1	New Year's Day (Celebrated from December 29 to January 3)
January 15	Adult's Day (Coming of Age Day)
February 11*	National Founding Day
March 21	Vernal Equinox Day
April 29*	Greenery Day
May 3*	Constitution Memorial Day
May 5	Children's Day
September 15	Respect-for-the-Aged Day
September 23*	Autumnal Equinox Day
October 10	Health-Sports Day
November 23	Labor Thanksgiving Day
December 23*	Emperor's Birthday

*Public holidays fall on the Monday when the original holiday is on a Sunday.

JAPAN

KEY CONTACTS

American Embassy Contacts

American Embassy Tokyo
10-1, Akasaka 1-chome
Minato-ku (107)
APO San Francisco 96503
 Tel: 81/3-224-5000
 Telex: 2422118 AMEMB J

Ambassador:	Michael H. Armacost
Deputy Chief of Mission:	L. Desaix Anderson
Political Section:	Rust M. Deming
Economic Section:	Aurelia E. Brazeal
Financial Attache:	Jon K. Hartzell
Commercial Section:	Keith R. Bovetti
Labor Officer:	John J. Lamazza
Consul (Consular Section):	M. Patricia Wazer
Federal Aviation Administration:	Edwin T. Kaneko
Administrative Section:	Jose J. Cao-Carcia
Regional Security Officer:	Bernd W. Schaumburg
Scientific Section:	Richard W. Getzinger
Agricultural Section:	Laverne Brabant
Public Affairs Officer:	Robert L. M. Nevitt
Agricultural Trade Office:	Laverne Brabant
Internal Revenue Service:	Dennis Tsujimoto
Customs Service:	Gary W. Waugh
Office of the Defense Attache:	Capt. Scott A. Van Hoften, U.S.N.

Business Contacts

Japanese Consulate
50 Fremont Street
San Francisco, CA 94105
 Tel: 415/777-3533

Japan External Trade Organization (JETRO)

San Francisco:
Quanta Building #501
360 Post Street
San Francisco, CA 94108
   Tel: 415/392-1333

New York:
McGraw-Hill Building, 44th Floor
1221 Avenue of the Americas
New York, NY 10020-1060
   Tel: 212/997-0400

Chicago:
401 North Michigan Avenue #660
Chicago, IL 60611
   Tel: 312/527-9000, 9177, 9119

Houston:
1221 McKinney
One Houston Center #1810
Houston, TX 77010
   Tel: 713/759-9595/7

Atlanta:
229 Peachtree Street NE #2011
Atlanta, GA 30303
   Tel: 404/681-0600

Los Angeles:
725 South Figueroa Street #1890
Los Angeles, CA 90071
   Tel: 213/624-8855

Denver:
1200 17th Street #1410
Denver, CO 80202
   Tel: 303/629-0404

Other Sources of Business Information

American Chamber of Commerce in Japan
Fukide Building #2
4-1-21, Toranomon
Minato-ku, Tokyo 105
    Tel: 81/3-433-5381
    Fax: 81/3/436-1446

Japan Chamber of Commerce and Industry
22-2, 3-chome
Marunouchi, Chiyoda-ku
Tokyo 100

Japan Information Service
845 North Michigan Avenue
Chicago, IL 60611

Japan High Tech Review
Christopher Mead, Publisher
P.O. Box 44952
Phoenix, AZ 85064
    Tel: 602/840-8277

Hotels in Tokyo

	Single (yen)	Double (yen)
Asakusa View Hotel Tel: 847-1111	14,000-15,000	25,000-28,000
Hilton Hotel Tel: 344-5111	24,000-34,000	29,000-40,000
Akasaka Tokyu Hotel Tel: 580-2311	18,000	26,000
Miyako Hotel Tokyo Tel: 447-3111	18,000	22,000
Century Hyatt Tokyo, The Tel: 349-0111	18,000	26,000/28,000
Le Pacific Meridien Tokyo Tel: 445-6711	19,000/21,000	22,000/25,000 29,000
Narita View Hotel Tel: 0476-32-1111	11,000	20,000

Imperial Hotel Tel: 504-1111	26,000	30,000
Hotel New Otani Tokyo Tel: 265-1111	20,000	26,000/29,500
Hotel IBIS Tel: 403-4411	13,000	19,500
Yaesu Fujiya Hotel Tel: 273-2111	9,500/11,000	17,000/22,000
Mitsui Urban Hotel Ginza Tel: 572-4131	14,000	19,000
Keio Plaza Inter-Continental Hotel Tel: 344-0111	18,500	23,000-32,000
Tokyo Marunouchi Hotel Tel: 215-2151	9,500/13,000	20,000/22,000
Ginza Marunouchi Hotel Tel: 543-5431	13,000	18,000
Ginza Kokusai Hotel Tel: 574-1121	11,892	16,995

Inexpensive Business Hotels

Hotel Juraku Tel: 251-7222	7,725	12,875
Tokyo Green Hotel Awajicho Tel: 255-4161	6,500	11,400
Tokyo Green Hotel Suidobashi Tel: 295-4161	7,000	12,000
Tokyo Green Hotel Korakuen Tel: 816-4161	7,000	15,000
Ikebukuro Center City Hotel Tel: 985-1311	6,684	11,216
Pearl Hotel Tel: 553-2211	7,700	12,400
City Pension Zem Tel: 661-0681	9,400	16,000

Business Hotel Motoharu Tel: 662-2394	5,300	
Shinjuku Weekly Mansion Tel: 354-1640	54,000/week 50,000 Security Deposit calculated exactly upon leaving/About 5,000 for gas and light expenses	
Shinjuku Town Hotel Tel: 365-2211	6,200	11,000
Shibuya Business Hotel Tel: 409-9300	7,930	11,550

Source: American Embassy in Tokyo (1990)

Market Research

One of the first steps in starting a business in Japan is to find out the condition of the Japanese market and how easy it will be to enter that market. Market research enterprises provide this information for American firms. Some research firms are listed below:

Nomura Research Institutes, Ltd.
Tel: 81-3-297-8100

Mitsubishi Research Institute, Inc.
Tel: 81-3-270-9211
Fax: 475-6343

Institute for Future Technology
Tel: 81-3-215-1911
Fax: 475-6343

InfoCom Research, Inc.
Tel: 81-3-470-7500
Fax: 475-7520

TIT Consult K.K.
Tel: 81-3-485-3280
Fax: 475-6343

English Language Periodicals Covering the Japanese Market

You may order the following periodicals from:

Japan Publications Trading Co., Ltd.
PO Box 5030 TOKYO International
Tokyo, Japan
    Tel: +81-3-292-3753
    Fax: +81-3-292-0410
    Telex: J27161 JPTCO

D=Daily	W=Weekly	BW=Biweekly	M=Monthly
BM=Bimonthly	A=Annually	SA=Semiannual	Q=Quarterly
V=Varies			

	Frequency/ U.S. Dollars
AEU: Journal of Asia Electronics Union	(BM,36)
Asahi Evening News	(D, 739)
Asian Medical Journal	(M, 84.50)
Atoms in Japan	(M, V)
Biomedical Research	(BM, 150)
Brain and Development	(BM, 110)
Bulletin of the Chemical Society of Japan	(M, 348)
Bulletin of Informatic and Cy Dernetic	(SA, 78)
Bulletin of Japan Society of Precision Engineering	(Q, 103.5)
Business Japan	(M, 102)
Business Tokyo	(M, 84)
Comerart	(M, 79)
Chemical and Pharmaceutical Bulletin	(M, V)
Chemistry Letters	(M, 186)
Civil Engineering in Japan	(A, V)
Commentarii Mathematic, Universitatis Sancti Pauli	(SA, 182)
Concrete Library, International	(SA, V)
Control-Theory and Advanced Technology	(Q, 130)
Cytologia-International Journal of Cytology	(Q, 205)
Daily Yomiuri	(D, 552)
Dental Materials Journal	(SA, 61)
Developing Economies	(Q, V)
Diamond's Japan Business Directly	(A, V)
DJIT-Digest of Japanese Industry and Technology	(7 annually, 221.5)
Economic Eye	(Q, 36.5)
Economic Survey of Japan	(A, V)

Factory Automation News	(17 annually, V)
Far Eastern Economic Review	(W, V)
Farming Japan	(BM, V)
Focus Japan	(M, 20+postage)
Food and Nutrition Bulletin	(Q, 30)
Foot Wear Press	(M, 210.5)
Geochemical Journal	(BM, 150)
Hitachi Review	(BM, 87.5)
Hitotsubashi Journal of Arts and Science	(A, V)
Hitotsubashi Journal of Economics	(SA, 48)
Hitotsubashi Journal of Law and Politics	(A, V)
Industria	(M, V)
Information and Communications in Japan Journal of Light and Visual Environment	(SA, V)
Journal of Nuclear Science and Technology	(M, 150)
Journal of the Operation Research Society of Japan	(Q, 147)
Journal of Space Technology and Science	(SA, V)
Journal of Textile Machinery Society of Japan	(Q, 63)
JSAE Review: Japanese Society of Automobile Engineering	(Q, 147.5)
Keio Journal of Medicine	(Q, 90)
Kitasato Archives of Experimental Medicine	(Q, 27.5)
Library and Information Science	(A, 66)
Mainichi Daily News	(D, 825)
Management Japan	(SA, 20)
MERI's Monthly Circular, Survey of Economic Condition in Japan	(M, 40)
Metalworking, Engineering and Marketing	(BM, 76.5)
Mitsubishi Electric Advance	(Q. 86.5)
Mitsubishi Heavy Industries Technical Review	(3 annually, 72.5)
Movie/TV Marketing	(M, 309)
National Technical Report	(BM, 104)
New Breeze (Quarterly of the ITU Association of Japan)	(Q, 45)
New Generation Computing	(Q, 269.5)
Nikkei High Tech Report	(SM, V)
Optoelectronics, Devices, and Technologies	(SA, 65)
Packaging Japan	(BM, 84)
Plastics Industry News	(M, 51+postage)
Polymer Journal	(M, 300)
Ports and Harbors	(M, 68)
Proceedings of Japan Academy	(10 annually, 135)
Proceedings of the Japan Congress on Material Research	(A, 150.5)

Proceedings of the Japan National Congress   (A, 202)
   for Applied Mechanics
Quarterly Forecast of Japan's Economy   (3 annually, 149)
Quarterly Report of the Railway   (Q, V)
   Technical Research Institute
Robot News   (M, V)
Science and Technology in Japan   (Q, 50+postage)
Scientific Papers of the Institute   (Q, V)
   of Physical and Chemical Research
Soils and Foundations   (Q, V)
Soil Science and Plant Nutrition   (Q, 80)
Techno Japan   (M, 226.5)
Telecom Tribune   (M, 50)
Terminal (Journal of Online Retrieval)   (Q, V)
Tokyo Business Today   (M, 72+postage)
Tokyo Journal   (M, V)
Transactions IEICE of Japan Sect.   (M, 120)
Transactions of IEE of Japan Sect.   (BM 85.5)
Transactions of the Iron and Steel Institute   (M, 380)
   of Japan
Transactions of the Japan Institute of Metals   (M, 240)
Transactions of Japan Society   (Q, 103.5)
   of Aeronautical and Space Science
Transactions of Japan Welding Society   (SA, V)
Wing Newsletter   (W,V)

Source: American Embassy in Tokyo (1990)

Airline Offices in Tokyo

Aeroflot (SU)   434-9671
Air France (AF)   475-1511
Air India (AI)   214-1981
Air Lanka (UL)   573-4261
Air Nauru (ON)   581-9271
Air New Zealand (TE)   287-1641
Air Pacific (FJ)   212-1351
Alitalia Airlines (AZ)   580-2181
All Nippon Airways (NH)   272-1212
American Airlines (AA)   214-2111
British Airways (BA)   593-8811
Canadian Airlines (CP)   281-7426
Cathay Pacific (CX)   504-1531

China Airlines (CI)	436-1661
Civil Aviation of China (CA)	505-2021
Continental (CO)	592-1631
Delta Airlines (DL)	213-8781
Dragon Airlines (KA)	589-5315
Garuda (GA)	593-1181
Iberia Airlines	582-3631
Iran Air (IR)	586-2101
Iraqi Airways (IA)	586-5801
Japan Air Lines (JL)	457-1111
Japan Air System (JD)	747-1515
Japan Asia Airways (EG)	455-7511
KLM (KL)	216-0771
Korean Air (KE)	211-3311
Lufthansa (LH)	580-2111
Malaysian Airlines (MH)	503-5961
Northwest (NW)	432-6000
Pakistan International (PK)	216-6511
Qantas Airways (QF)	212-1351
Savena (SN)	585-6151
SAS (SK)	503-8101
Singapore Airlines (SQ)	213-3431
Swissair (SR)	212-1016
United Airlines (UA)	817-4411
UTA (UT)	593-0773
Varig (RG)	211-6751

Source: American Embassy, Tokyo (1990)

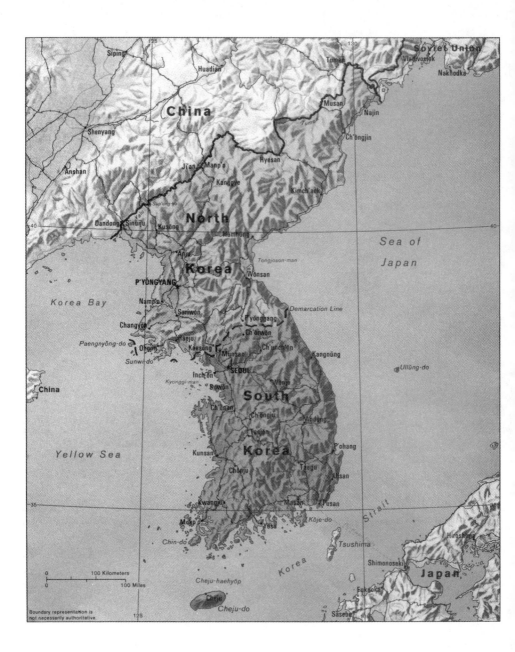

KOREA

KOREA
In a Nutshell

		Urban Population
Population (1992)	43,200,000	65.6%

Main Urban Areas		Percentage of Total
Seoul	10,500,000	24.3
Pusan	3,650,700	8.4
Taegu	2,000,200	4.6
Inchon	1,600,000	3.7

Land Area	38,031 square miles
	98,500 square kilometers
Comparable European State	Slightly larger than Portugal
Comparable U.S. State	Slightly smaller than Indiana
Language	Korean
Common Business Language	English
Currency	South Korean won (1W = 100 chon)
Best Air Connection	Los Angeles-Seoul (daily)
	Asiana Airlines 800/227-4262
	New York-Anchorage-Seoul (daily)
	Los Angeles-Seoul (daily)
	Korea Air 800/223-1155
	San Francisco-Seoul (Mon., Tues., Wed., Fri., Sat.)
	United Airlines 800/538-2929
Best Hotel	Hyatt Regency
	($216/night as of 2/92)

CHAPTER CONTENTS

INTRODUCTION

Economic Overview

In the past 20 years, the Republic of Korea has transformed from an underdeveloped, mainly agrarian, country into a major industrial power. The change is largely attributable to the Korean government's industrial policies and programs.

Korea's economy is export-led, leaving the country vulnerable to world price fluctuations. Thus, this economy was relatively hard-hit by the oil shocks of the 1970s. However, it was able to post a 9% to 10% annual real growth rate throughout most of the decade.

The sustained expansion that propelled Korea into its current prosperity began in 1982. Despite the recession of the early 1980s, Korea managed 8.5% annual growth rate from 1981 to 1985. The period from 1986 to 1988 proved even more prosperous, with average annual growth rates over 12%.

Recent revaluation of the won, Korea's currency, and rising labor costs hurt export competitiveness and slowed expansion to 7.5% annually in 1989 and 1990. Korea's Economic Planning Board projected GNP growth of 7.5% for 1991 and 1992.

Korea's exports in 1988 surpassed $60 billion (a 27% increase from 1987), while imports ran almost $52 billion. However, exports grew by only 2% in 1989 and imports rose 7.5%, cutting the trade surplus to $4.6 billion.

Approximately one-third of Korea's gross domestic product is generated by exports. The Sixth Five-Year Plan recommends concentrating on high value-added and high technology industries to sustain export growth. To achieve this end, several industries have been targeted for increasing investment and technological upgrading, including machinery, electronics, specialty chemicals, and automobiles.

The nation's per capita income reached $4,834 in 1989, up sharply from $1,392 in 1978 and $250 in 1970. The per capita income was forecasted to reach $5,000 by the end of 1991. Korea has an economically active population that is expected to increase by 2.4% annually. Currently, the workforce includes 17 million of the 43 million Koreans.

Inflation has not been a problem, running at 2.6% in 1988 and 3.5% in 1989. Some economists worry that inflation may rise relatively higher than Korea's trading partners due to the consistent current account surpluses. Inflation for 1990 was 6.7%.

Consumer Demand

Changes in Korean consumption is attributable to several factors, including increased income levels, social and cultural change, and changes in consumer lifestyles. Westernization and the increasing influence of mass media have also been major forces of change. With improvements in household income, there has been an increase in the consumption of high-quality foods and, paradoxically, an increase in processed "instant foods" and fast foods. Meanwhile, there has been a decline in rice and barley consumption. Also, as Korean living conditions have improved, the demand for services such as education, travel, health services, and communications has risen. Educational and training tapes, travel and tourism, exercise equipment, and health care are rapidly growing markets.

Korea has also shown a steep upturn in demand for consumer durables such as passenger cars, color televisions, VCRs, refrigerators, washing machines, etc. As Korean society has developed, segmentation is practiced more widely by businesses, leading to retail organizations specializing in products for consumers with certain demographic profiles. The development of Korean society has also exposed consumers to alternative marketing and financing. The introduction of catalog sales and direct mail coupled with credit card financing has added a new twist to marketing in Korea.

Trade Flows

Korean trade with the United States totaled $30 billion in 1988, with Korea holding a $9.5 billion surplus. The United States is the second largest exporter to Korea, behind only Japan, while Korea is America's seventh-largest trading partner. Major U.S. export items include: hides and skins, corn, aircraft, cotton, steel and iron scrap, wood, ADP machines, and electronics components.

The U.S. Department of Commerce suggests numerous export prospects for the Korean market, including computers, software, medical equipment, telecommunications equipment, pollution control equipment, scientific instruments, construction machinery, and food processing equipment.

In 1989, Korea's exports were divided as follows:

United States	35.3%
Japan	19.8%
EC	13.4%
Other	31.5%

Its imports for 1989 were divided as follows:

Japan	30.7%
United States	24.6%
EC	11.7%
Other	33.0%

Policies to Attract New Business

Over the past several years, the Korean government has implemented a number of actions aimed at liberalizing the economy and achieving more foreign investment — reducing the current account surplus and decreasing government intervention. Actions to achieve these objectives have included such aggressive measures as revaluing the won, current tariffs, eliminating the import surveillance system, and placing a majority of manufactured items on the automatic approved list of imports.

The Korean government views long-term stability as the key to attracting new ventures and consequently has promoted policies targeting optimal economic growth, price stability, stabilization of labor-management relations, and liberalization of financial markets. Korea has devoted considerable energies toward further development of its securities market.

Moreover, the Korean government has moved to reduce its direct influences on the economy by partially privatizing a number of state-owned corporations. Also, the government has relaxed exchange laws to allow trade contracts to be denominated in won, the local currency. Korea has also established two free export zones, the Iri and Masan zones, in which imported materials can be processed into finished goods without duty or tax.

Finally, the Foreign Capital Inducement Law (FCIL) was simplified in 1987 to attract additional foreign capital. The amended FCIL allows access to a wider range of industries, and it significantly simplifies the application and approval process.

APPROACHING THE MARKET

Trade and Investment Decision-Making Infrastructure

Korea's government has played an indispensable role in the economic development of the country. It has undertaken an export-driven approach for its economy and consequently has promoted policies to ensure rapid growth of exports. As the economy has become increasingly complex and Korean society more democratic, the government has become less interventionist and has yielded to the interests of labor, business, students, and others.

Korea welcomes foreign investment and trade. Thus, in past years, it has streamlined the decision-making process regarding foreign businesses and transactions with these entities. The Korean Ministry of Finance is best suited to assist foreign business people concerned with initial investigations and application processes. Inquiries should be directed to the Investment Promotion Division in Seoul (Tel: 503-9276).

Consulting Services

It is highly recommended that the prospective investor or trader research their market area of business with both the Korean and U.S. governments.

Korean Government

The Republic of Korea maintains an embassy in the United States at: 2370 Massachusetts Avenue, N.W., Washington, D.C. 20008 (Tel: 202/939-5600). Korea also maintains Consulate Generals in Anchorage, Chicago, Honolulu, Houston, Los Angeles, New York, San Francisco, Atlanta, and Seattle.

The Korea Trade Promotion Corporation manages Korean Trade Centers at the following locations:

460 Park Avenue
Suite 402
New York, NY 10022
Tel: 212/826-0900

2050 Stemmons Freeway
Room 155
Dallas, TX 75258
Tel: 214/748-9341

111 East Wacker Drive
Suite 519
Chicago, IL 60601
Tel: 312/644-4323

One Biscayne Tower
Suite 3669
Miami, FL 33131
Tel: 305/374-4648

700 South Flower Street
Suite 3220
Los Angeles, CA 90017
Tel: 213/627-9426

Washington Liaison Office
1030 15th Street, N.W.
Suite 752
Washington, D.C. 20005
Tel: 202/333-2040

The Export-Import Bank of Korea is located at the following address:

New York Representative Office
20th Floor
Hahn Kook Center Building
460 Park Avenue
New York, NY 10022
Tel: 212/355-7280

U.S. Government

General information concerning the Korean market, economic trends, commercial developments, production, and trade may be obtained from the Office of Pacific Basin, Room 2308, International Trade Administration, U.S. Department of Commerce, Washington, D.C. 20230. The Commerce Department also offers the Agent/Distributor Service for a fee.

The U.S. is also represented by an embassy at 82 Sejoug-ro, Chongro-ku, Seoul (Tel: 732-2601 through 2618). The foreign commercial staff of the embassy is available to assist American business people.

Sales Promotion, Fairs, and Conferences

The following is a list of the major Korean Trade Promotion Corporation (KOTRA)-sponsored fairs and exhibitions.

- Seoul International Trade Fair
- Korea Electronic Parts & Equipment International Show
- Seoul International Food Technology Exhibition
- Seoul International Instrumentation Exhibition
- Korean Auto Parts & Accessories Exhibition
- Seoul International Toy Fair

Several other non-KOTRA affiliated fairs take place annually, such as the Seoul International Computers and Video Equipment Show, the Seoul International Machine Tool Show, and the Seoul International Motor Show.

Advertising

In 1988, advertising expenditures for Korean firms reached $1.87 billion, an increase of 31.5% over the previous year. The breakdown of ad expenditure share by media follows:

Newspaper	36.2%
Television	34.8%
Magazine	5.1%
Radio	4.0%
Overseas	2.1%

There are 23 major daily newspapers in Korea, 13 of which are in Seoul (yet circulate nationwide). The four major newspapers, with an individual circulation of over one-half million, are *Dong-A Ilbo*, *Chasun Ilbo*, *Han Kook Ilbo*, and *Joong Ang Ilbo*. Rates in the larger newspapers vary for a centimeter-wide single column from a high of 75,000 won to a low of 38,000 won.

Television is becoming an increasingly important advertising medium. At the outset of 1988 there were roughly 9.6 million television sets, most of which were color sets. Prime time runs from 8:30 p.m. to 10:30 p.m., and rates charged by either of the two Korean broadcasting companies range from 3.15 million to 3.4 million won for a 30-second spot.

Radio advertising is the third most common advertising medium, reaching almost 30 million radios throughout Korea in 1988. There are 54 radio stations (five F.M. and 47 relay stations). Radio prime time runs from 7:00 a.m. to 1:00 p.m. and the rate for a 20-second spot in Seoul runs from 219,000 to 442,700 won.

As of mid-1988, Korea had 2,163 periodicals in monitored circulation, many aimed at women. Rates in the leading magazine for a single-page color advertisement with an offset picture runs between 1.6 million to 2.3 million won. All motion picture houses project advertising strips or stills ranging in length from 30 seconds to two minutes, in either color or black and white.

Agents and Distributors

A firm wishing to enter the Korean market has several alternatives. First, the firm can establish a branch sales office managed by home office personnel. The firm may choose to appoint one of the U.S. trading firms in Korea as their representative. Alternatively, a registered Korean trading firm may be utilized on an exclusive or nonexclusive basis. Frequently, foreign suppliers will combine these alternatives. The U.S. Department of Commerce offers help and advice through the Agent and Distributor Service (ADS) for a nominal fee (depending on the number of qualified partners sought and the degree of customization in the search).

By law, only registered traders are authorized to import goods in their own names, with exceptions in cases involving goods imported in connection with foreign private investment, goods imported by select organizations, or goods for Korean government procurement.

Trading licenses are issued by the Korean government. A growing number of manufacturing firms export their products and are registered traders due to economies of scale and the desire to avoid paying a middleman. Presently there are eight General Trading Companies (GTCs), handling imports and exports for the major Korean conglomerates. The GTCs do handle independent clients (other than their manufacturing arm, that is). However, the large trading firms may not be able to devote as much attention to individual clients as some of the smaller, more personalized trading firms can. On the other hand, the larger firms may be in a better position to extend credit or bring a particular deal to close by enhanced credibility or contacts.

There are 4,156 offer-agents or commission-agents registered with the Association of Foreign Trading Agents of Korea (AFTAK), 44 of which are from the United States. These firms act as representatives of foreign manufacturers and suppliers and make offers on behalf of their principals. Offer agents may provide the most efficient representation if your company feels it will be selling to large organizations or conglomerates with their own trading arm that will handle the import paperwork.

Setting Up Business Operations

Firms interested in setting up a branch office in Korea must apply to the Bank of Korea for approval. If the firm intends to repatriate funds, it must obtain authorization from the Bank of Korea to start operations. If repatriation is not intended, then notification and registration is all that is necessary. The Ministry of Finance, as well as the Bank of Korea, must approve the establishment of foreign corporations in Korea.

The following foreign operations must meet with Ministry of Finance approval:

- banking or financing operations
- securities underwriting
- insurance
- funds management services

INVESTMENT CLIMATE

The government of Korea is selling shares of many state-owned enterprises as a means of attracting new capital, although bidding is not currently open to foreign investors. Nonetheless, Korea's privatization and general nonintervention policy has been implemented and adhered to, with general satisfaction from the investment community.

Dispute Resolution

The Korean government regulations stipulate that parties involved in an international commercial dispute attempt to settle differences immediately and amicably.

The Korean business tradition stresses compromise and scorns litigation. There are, however, several local law firms handling the legal affairs of international companies. The Commercial Section of the American Embassy in Seoul will provide a list of lawyers upon request. Korea is a member of the International Commercial Arbitration Association. In Korea, a firm may submit a complaint or dispute to the Korean Commercial Arbitration Board.

The Korean government adopted a negative list system for foreign investment approvals, whereby all areas are open to investment, except those on the negative list. Of the 1,048 sectors recognized under the Korean standard industrial classification system (SIC), 211 sectors are presently included on the negative list — 51 sectors are classified as "prohibited" and 160 are "restricted." Prohibited sectors include manufacture of tobacco products, newspaper and book publication, electric power, operation of bars and saloons, radio and television broadcasting, gambling, and postal and telecom services.

The restricted list covers areas where the government is interested in foreign investment only if certain conditions are met. Usually, these conditions boil down to a joint venture in which the foreign participant contributes cash and the Korean partner contributes land or machinery. The restricted list includes projects that require specific government assistance, produce pollution, and depend heavily on energy and other imported materials. Examples are dairy operations, food processing and distribution, livestock breeding, and mining.

Under the revised FCIL, the Bank of Korea has the authority to approve foreign investment without prior consultations with other ministries (automatic approval) if the foreign equity investment is less than 50%. Between 1989 and 1993, Korea will gradually expand the list of investments eligible for the automatic approval process.

VISITING AND LOCATING

Visas

Visitors should have a valid passport and visa to enter Korea. Visas are issued by any Korean diplomatic or consular post. Two types of visas are issued: temporary (valid for 90 days and usually issued for business travelers and tourists) and nontemporary (for stays longer than 90 days). Visitors staying 15 days or less need not obtain a visa (except for Japanese nationals). Currently, no vaccination certificate is required under Korea's quarantine regulations.

Currency

Foreigners and Koreans may carry Korean won into or out of the country, as long as the amount does not exceed W2 million. Foreigners may carry any amount of foreign currency into Korea, but amounts above $5,000 must be declared. Prior to departure, visitors may convert won back to foreign exchange, up to the value of $100, at any authorized foreign exchange bank. Korea has 886 banks authorized to deal in foreign exchange. These independent banks are now able to carry on international transactions with correspondent banks.

Etiquette and Language

Business etiquette is largely derived from traditional Korean conservativism and work ethic. This style emphasizes harmony and structure over innovation and experimentation. The Korean language is very difficult to learn and, thus, a translator is highly recommended unless one is certain of the English proficiency of the Korean with whom dealings are being conducted. Although many natives speak English, Korean is the language of the country. Consequently, promotional literature and instructions are acceptable in English, but preferable in Korean. Meetings can generally be conducted in English.

First names or nicknames should not be used. It is appropriate to use job titles, such as vice-president, director, or manager. Social titles, such as Mr., Mrs., or Ms., are also correct.

To avoid confusion, do not use the word "not" when phrasing a question. Remember that favorable responses may only signify courtesy, and one should be prepared to wait for a final answer. It is good practice to follow up a meeting with a written summary.

Punctuality is highly stressed in Korean business relations, as an early or tardy arrival may disrupt an otherwise full business schedule. Business cards are customary and reflect the identity, position, and status of the presenter.

There is normally a seating protocol, and the person seated in the chair at the head of the table is usually the top-ranking executive. Seating the highest-ranking officials or top negotiators in the middle of the conference table — Reagan style — has not caught on yet. It is advised to ask where to sit in a meeting.

Unlike the Western emphasis on written contracts and the concept of "buyer beware," Koreans prefer loosely structured yet flexible contracts and agreements. Consequently, parties to a contract must clarify their obligations.

Holidays and Hours of Operation

Korean business and government offices recognize the following statutory holidays:

January 1-3	New Year Celebration
March 1	Independence Day
Lunar (April 5)	Buddha's Birthday
July 17	Children's Day
August 15	Liberation Day
Lunar (August 15)	Thanksgiving
October 1	Armed Forces Day
October 3	Founder's Day
October 9	Hongul Day
December 25	Christmas Day

Normal working hours for both government and businesses are 9:00 a.m. to 5:00 p.m. weekdays and 9:00 a.m. to 1:00 p.m. on Saturday. The schedule for service establishments (department stores, shops, restaurants, etc.) vary as in the United States.

KOREA

KEY CONTACTS

American Embassy Contacts

American Embassy Seoul
82 Sejong-Ro
Chongro-ku
APO San Francisco 96301
    Tel: 82/2-732-2601 thru 18
    Telex: AMEMB 23108
    Fax: 82/2-738-8845

Ambassador:	Donald P. Gregg
Charge d'Affaires:	Thomas S. Brooks
Political Section:	Charles Kartman
Economic Section:	Kevin J. McGuire
Commercial Section:	Peter Frederick
Consul (Consular Section):	Edward H. Wilkinson
Administrative Section:	Robert G. Deason
Regional Security Officer:	Paul D. Sorensen
Scientific Section:	Kenneth D. Cohen
Immigration and Naturalization Officer:	Donald Whitney
Agricultural Section:	George J. Pope
Agricultural Trade Office:	Howard R. Wetzel
Public Affairs Officer:	John M. Reid
Customs Service:	Calvin G. White
Military Assistance Advisory Group:	Bg. Fred N. Halley, U.S.A.
Office of the Defense Attache:	Col. James V. Young, U.S.A.
Drug Enforcement Agency:	David Surh
Internal Revenue Service:	Dennis Tsujimoto (resident in Tokyo)

Business Contacts

Embassy, the Republic of Korea
Lee, Jong-Soon, Attache
2600 Virginia Avenue, NW
Watergate Hotel Suite 200
Washington, DC 20039
   Tel: 202/939-6478

Korea Trade Center
Min Ha Hwang, Manager
1129 20th Street, NW #410
Washington, DC 20036
   Tel: 202/857-7919/21
   Fax: 202/857-7923

Korea Foreign Trade Association

New York:
460 Park Avenue #555
New York, NY 10022
   Tel: 212/421-8804
   Fax: 212/223-3827

Washington, DC:
1030 15th Street, NW
Washington, DC 20005
   Tel: 202/686-1550

Korea Trade Promotion Corporation

Washington, DC:
1030 15th Street, NW
Washington, DC 20005
   Tel: 202/333-2040
   Fax: 202/898-1673

New York:
460 Park Avenue #402
New York, NY 10022
   Tel: 212/826-0900
   Telex: 649404 KTC NYK
   Fax: 212/888-4930

Los Angeles:
700 South Flower Street #3220
Los Angeles, CA 90017
   Tel: 213/627-9426/9
   Fax: 213/627-6404

Chicago:
111 East Wacker Drive #519
Chicago, IL 60601
   Tel: 312/644-4323/4
   Fax: 312/644-4879

Dallas:
World Trade Center #155
2050 Stemmons Freeway
Dallas, TX 75258-0023
   Tel: 214/748-9341/2
   Fax: 214/748-4630

Miami:
1 Biscayne Tower
Suite 3669
Miami, FL 33131
   Tel: 305/374-4648
   Fax: 305/375-9332

Branch Offices of U.S. Commercial Banks

American Express Bank	2-753-2435
Bank of America	2-733-2455
Bank of California	2-736-5431
Bank of Hawaii	2-757-0831
Bankers Trust Co	2-778-9010
Chase Manhattan	2-758-5114
Chemical Bank	2-778-8951
Citibank (Downtown)	2-731-1114
Citibank (It'aewon)	2-792-2000
Citibank (Yongdong)	2-540-3907
First Interstate of California	2-733-8681
First National Bank of Boston	2-733-6980
First National Bank of Chicago	2-753-8980
Irving Trust	2-774-1441
Manufacturers Hanover	2-778-5411
Security Pacific National Bank	2-757-6850

Source: Korea National Tourism Corporation (1990)

Air Service to Seoul From the United States

Route	Flight Time (Hours:Minutes)	Business Class Fare (Roundtrip)
Delta Airlines		
Portland-Seoul	11:30	$2,058
Korea Air		
L.A.-Seoul	13:00	$1,892
L.A.-Tokyo-Seoul	14:50	$1,892
L.A.-Honolulu-Seoul	18:00	$1,892
Honolulu-Seoul	11:00	$1,570
NYC-Anchorage-Seoul	17:00	$2,472
United Airlines		
Honolulu-Seoul	11:00	$1,570
San Francisco-Seoul	12:49	$1,892
L.A.-Seoul	13:25	$1,892
Northwest Airlines		
Detroit-Seoul	15:10	$2,474
Honolulu-Seoul	11:00	$1,570
L.A.-Seoul	13:25	$1,892
Seattle-Seoul	11:40	$1,892

Source: The airlines cited as of December 1990.

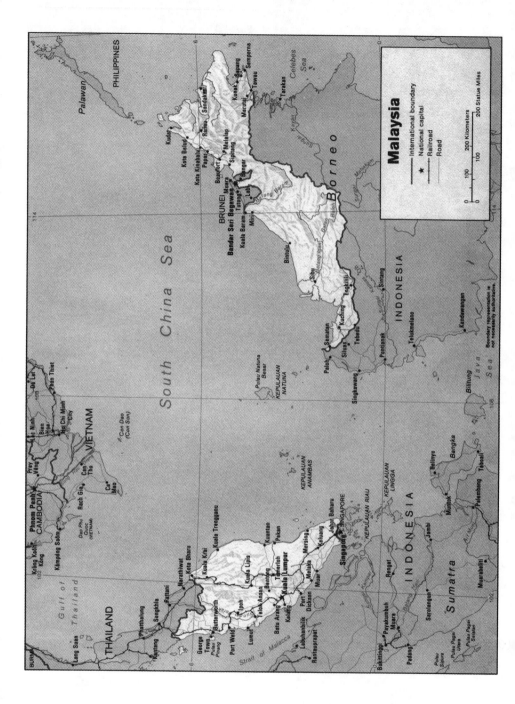

MALAYSIA

MALAYSIA
In a Nutshell

		Urban Population
Population (1992)	18,300,000	40.3%

Main Urban Areas		Percentage of Total
Kuala Lumpur	1,000,000	5.4
George Town	300,000	1.6
Ipoh	275,000	1.5

Land Area	128,328 square miles
	332,370 square kilometers

Comparable European State	Slightly smaller than Finland
Comparable U.S. State	Slightly larger than New Mexico

Language	*Peninsular Malaysia* — Malay, English, Chinese dialects, Tamil *Sabah* — English, Malay, Mandarin, Hakka *Sarawak* — English, Malay, Mandarin, tribal dialects
Common Business Language	English
Currency	ringgit (1M$ = 100 sen)
Best Air Connection	Los Angeles-Tokyo-Kuala Lumpur (Mon., Fri., Sat.) Los Angeles-Honolulu-Taipei-Kuala Lumpur (Sun., Wed., Fri.) Malaysia Air 800/421-8641
Best Hotel	Hyatt Kinabalu (business district) ($144/night as of 2/92)

CHAPTER CONTENTS

INTRODUCTION AND REGIONAL ORIENTATION

Socioeconomic Indicators and Conditions

Since its independence in 1957, Malaysia's economy has been transformed from a colonial producer of rubber and tin into a modern, diversified economy in which agriculture, industry, mining, and the service sector all play important roles. From 1965 to 1984, the economy experienced diversification and a period of sustained rapid growth (averaging 7% to 8%). Manufacturing grew in importance, supplanting agriculture as the economy's largest sector. In 1989, manufacturing accounted for 25.3% of real GDP, agriculture 20.16%, services 17.9%, mining (including petroleum) 10.4%, construction 3.2%, government services 11.3%, and utilities 1.9%.

The collapse of commodity prices in 1985 to 1986 (particularly petroleum and palm oil) led to a sharp recession. Nominal GNP declined by a total of 11.5% in two years; real GDP was unchanged.

Improved commodity prices and strong growth in manufactured exports since 1987 have helped the economy recover from the recession. Nominal GNP grew 12.6% and real GDP was 8.5% in 1989. Total GNP in 1989 was approximately M $97 billion. Inflation was 2.8% and the current account was M $400 million in deficit. Unemployment has declined since the recession to reach 7.5% of the labor force of 6.83 million.

Malaysia is the world's largest producer of rubber and palm oil, the fourth largest in cocoa, and the leading exporter of tropical timber. It is also a significant producer and exporter of petroleum and liquefied natural gas. Industry is dominated by the production of electronic components, telecommunications equipment, electrical machinery, and textiles and apparel. Malaysia is the third largest producer of semiconductor devices after the United States and Japan.

The Malaysian economy is relatively open with total exports and imports of goods and services equal to 133% of GNP. Malaysia's leading exports in 1989 included the following:

- electronic components (US $3.8 billion)
- petroleum (US $ 2.9 billion)
- timber products (US $ 2.7 billion)
- palm oil products (US $2.0 billion)
- rubber (US $1.4 billion)
- textiles and apparel (US $1.1 billion)
- telecommunications equipment (US $3.9 billion)

The New Economic Policy (NEP) was established in 1971 with two objectives: (1) to eradicate poverty in Malaysia and (2) to restructure the economy to end the identification of economic function with race. In particular, the NEP was designed to enhance the economic standing of the ethnic Malays and other indigenous peoples (collectively known as "bumiputras" in Malay). Rapid growth during the 1970s and early 1980s made it possible to expand the share of the economy for bumiputras without reducing the economic attainments of the other groups.

One important NEP goal is to alter the pattern of ownership of corporate equity in Malaysia. The NEP seeks to ensure that at least 30% of corporate equity is held by bumiputras, 40% by other Malaysians (primarily Chinese and Indian Malaysians), and no more than 30% by non-Malaysians. To this end, the government established various trusts which provided government funds to purchase foreign-owned shareholdings in market transactions, on behalf of the bumiputra population. Foreign firms (often 100% foreign owned) have been urged to restructure their equity in line with the NEP guidelines. As of 1985, the government estimated that bumiputras held 18% of corporate equity, nonbumiputra Malaysians (including the government) 56%, and foreign residents 26%. It is generally acknowledged now that the equity goals of the NEP cannot be achieved by 1990. The government has implicitly recognized this fact, adopting more pragmatic guidelines for foreign investors and permitting two foreign firms to restructure without meeting the strict NEP guidelines.

Finance and Investment Policies

The Malaysian government's attitude toward foreign investment is largely dependent on the type of investment, when the investment was made, and the extent to which there is Malaysian and bumiputra participation in the investment. Despite the NEP goal of limiting foreign ownership of incorporated businesses to 30% by the year 1990, the government encourages foreign investment.

The government maintains a favorable climate for foreign investment in Malaysia in manufacturing and agroindustrial enterprises to meet the country's economic development goals. Malaysia's investment incentives are competitive with those of other countries. The government has established the Malaysian Industrial Development Authority (MIDA) to promote foreign investment in Malaysia. MIDA works with both foreign and domestic investors in developing their proposals, processing investment applications, and coordinating permits and licenses.

In 1986, the government decided to actively seek increased foreign investment. In part, this desire was prompted by the 1985 to 1986 recession and a renewed emphasis on the private sector as the "engine of growth." As a result, the government has significantly liberalized its regulations affecting foreign investment in a number of areas. Guidelines on foreign equity participation were liberalized in 1986 along with access to credit markets, foreign exchange controls, and the ability of foreign firms to acquire land.

Policies to Attract New Business

Investment Incentives and Privileges

Malaysia provides a number of tax incentives to investors, both foreign and Malaysian. These incentives have been modified over time, most recently in the Promotion of Investments Act 1986. The principal investment incentives are Pioneer Status and Investment Tax Allowance. An enterprise may qualify for one or the other of these incentives, but not both. Normally, an investor will be accorded the one that is most beneficial to the particular enterprise. These two incentives are available to investors in manufacturing, agriculture, and tourism.

Pioneer status. This incentive provides 100% relief from Malaysian income tax and development tax for a period of five years from the start of operations. The tax relief period may be extended for an additional five years if the company meets certain criteria established by the Ministry of Trade and Industry. For integrated agricultural enterprises, pioneer status may be extended only for the processing portion of the investment.

Investment tax allowance. This incentive exempts a company from Malaysian income tax and development tax equal to an agreed percentage of qualifying capital expenditures (up to 100%) incurred during a period of up to five years from the start of operations.

In addition, Malaysia provides a number of other incentives to encourage manufacturing and agricultural investments. Some of these include the following:

- Location Incentive - provides for a 5% abatement of taxable income for up to five years for enterprises locating in designated "promoted industrial areas" (manufacturing only).
- Small-scale Incentive - provides for a 5% abatement of taxable income for up to five years for enterprises with a paid-up capital less than M $500,000 (manufacturing only).
- Equity/Employment Incentive - provides for a 5% abatement of taxable income for up to five years for enterprises which newly comply with the government's equity or employment guidelines in 1986 or later (manufacturing and agriculture).

- Abatement of Adjusted Income for Exports - provides for an abatement of adjusted income equal to 50% of the proportion of sales represented by exports. (This applies to manufacturing and certain processed agricultural products.)

- Export Allowance - an export allowance of 5% of the FOB value of export sales is granted to trading companies exporting products manufactured in Malaysia. (This applies to manufacturing and certain processed agricultural products.)

- Double Deduction for Export Credit Insurance Premiums - provides a double deduction from income for export credit insurance premium paid to a company approved by the Ministry of Finance (manufacturing and agriculture).

- Double Deduction for Promotion of Exports - provides for a double deduction from income for expenses of overseas advertising, export market research, preparation of tenders for sales abroad, supply of technical information abroad, supply of free samples abroad, participation in overseas trade shows approved by the Ministry of Trade and Industry, public relations services abroad, overseas travel expenses, and maintaining overseas sales offices (manufacturing and industries).

- Research and Development Incentive - provides that research and development expenses in projects approved by the Ministry of Finance are eligible for double deduction from income. In addition, equipment used in approved research is eligible for capital allowances (manufacturing and agriculture).

- Double Deduction for Training - provides for a double deduction from income for expenses for approved training (manufacturing only).

- Tariff Protection - tariff protection can be granted to industries in a position to supply a major portion of the domestic market. Such protection will be based on the degree of utilization of local raw materials, the level of local value added, and the level of technology transferred. The level of such tariff protection will be reviewed from time to time. In addition, Malaysia may grant temporary protection in the form of quantitative import restrictions. (This applies to manufacturing and agriculture.)

- Exemption from Customs Duties on Raw Materials/Components - exemptions will be granted for enterprises manufacturing for export where such raw materials/components are not manufactured locally or, if manufactured locally, are not of acceptable quality. Full or partial exemption may be granted to enterprises producing for the domestic market under certain conditions.

- Exemption from Customs Duties on Machinery and Equipment - exemption is normally granted where the machinery is not produced locally.

Free Trade Zones/Special Economic Zones

Free trade zones (FTZs) are areas designed for manufacturing companies producing or assembling products principally or wholly for export. Customs controls are minimal, and all machinery and raw materials and components directly used in production may be imported duty free. Malaysia established nine FTZs under the Free Trade Zone Act of 1971. They are largely administered by the state economic development corporations of the states in which they are located, which currently include Penang, Malacca, Selangor, and Johore. Both foreign and domestic firms may locate in FTZs and are eligible for the full range of investment incentives offered by the Malaysian government. In order to locate in a FTZ, a firm must export at least 80% of its output, and any production to be sold in Malaysia is subject to normal customs duties.

Malaysia also has a number of licensed manufacturing warehouses (LMWs) to enable companies to establish factories mainly for the export market in areas where establishment of an FTZ is not practical. In effect, a single factory site can become a miniature FTZ.

Labuan Island, off the state of Sabah, and Langkawi Island, off the state of Kedah, are Malaysia's only free ports. Acquired from Sabah by the federal government in 1983, Labuan is the site of several healthy industries based on Sabah's extensive offshore gas deposits. Langkawi became a free port in 1987, and most of its development has been in the tourist industry.

APPROACHING THE MARKET

State and Private Services

Market Research

Market research is recognized as an essential and effective marketing tool in Malaysia that is used with increasing frequency and with very satisfactory results. Several firms, including Asian ones, supply this service and have developed an acceptable competence in professional market research. These firms are constantly expanding their activities to meet the growing demand for their expertise. Market research firms based in Singapore and Hong Kong also take on commissions in Malaysia.

Although professional market investigation services are available, many local trading firms conduct market inquiries on a rule-of-thumb basis. While the results are often good, they vary according to the competence of the firms and the staffs responsible for market planning and development. Business organizations, both government and private, may also be helpful as sources of market information.

There are several chambers of commerce organized on an ethnic basis. They have good membership support and are loosely tied into a single united chamber in an effort to achieve a consolidated approach when representing the viewpoint of private enterprise in its relations with the government. The largest chambers have been organized by ethnic Chinese business people and are located in Kuala Lumpur, Ipoh, and Penang. Membership includes a large number of importers and exporters.

Setting Up Business Operations

Forms of Business Organization

Three types of companies may be incorporated under the Companies Act: a company limited by shares, a company limited by guarantee, and an unlimited company with or without share capital.

In a company limited by shares, the liability of a member is limited to a specific amount undertaken. In a company limited by guarantee, the liability of members is limited to a specified amount undertaken to be contributed to assets on the company's termination. An unlimited company has no limit on the liability of the members and resembles a general partnership in this respect.

Private companies, denoted as "Sendirian Berhad" or "Sdn. Bhd.," may be limited or unlimited. A private limited company restricts the right to transfer its shares, limits its membership to no more than 50, prohibits public subscription to its shares, and prohibits invitation to the public to deposit money with the company for fixed periods or payable by call.

Public limited companies, denoted as "Berhad" or "Bhd.," are companies whose shares may be offered to the public for subscription. Companies may apply to the stock exchange for permission to have their share listed.

Companies incorporated outside Malaysia that do business in Malaysia are classed as foreign companies by the Companies Act. Before local establishment, a foreign company is required to deposit the following with the Companies Registry:

1. a certified copy of its certificate of incorporation

2. a certified copy of the charter, statues and/or articles of the company that define its constitution

3. a list of its directors and secretary

4. a memorandum of appointment stating the names and addresses of two or more persons resident in Malaysia authorized to act legally and responsibly on the company's behalf

Partnerships and sole proprietorships must register with the Registration of Businesses before they can begin to operate. There is a registration fee and an annual renewal fee. All companies must register with the Registrar of Companies by submitting to them the following forms:

1. Memorandum and Articles of Association

2. Statutory declaration of compliance with the Companies Act

3. Certificate of identity

4. Consent to act as director

5. Statutory declaration by persons before appointments as directors

Companies pay registration fees based on the amount of authorized capital. Both filing and stamping fees apply for submission of the above documents.

The Companies Act requires that the secretary and a minimum of two directors must have their principal or only place of residence in Malaysia, and company auditors must be approved by the Malaysian government.

Sales Promotion, Fairs, Conferences, and Advertising

Advertising is widely used as a sales tool in Malaysia. There are several advertising and public relations firms that will assist the U.S. exporter and his or her agent in media presentations. The most effective media advertising is done in the daily newspaper. These publications have a wide circulation and reach readers in the major local languages. While Malay is the national language, most of the business community can be reached in the English language press. The principal English language newspapers are the *New Straits Times* and the *Sunday Times*. Other publications include the *Malay Mail*, the *Asian Wall Street Journal*, and *Business Times*.

Advertising in American publications also reaches the Malaysian market. U.S. consumer and trade journals have a wide circulation — often reaching a worldwide readership, particularly among the more affluent business and professional customers, many of whom are headquartered in Malaysia.

Radio and television are increasingly used by distributors to advertise consumer goods. Rising family incomes make these media very popular methods of advertising. The majority of the population listens daily to Malaysian radio broadcasts. Television operates over three channels offering a full range of programming. Both radio and television offer commercial spots.

Transportation and Freight (Air/Sea)

The Malaysian government attaches considerable importance to the accommodation of international air flights and to the expansion of domestic aviation. In 1988, the government-owned Malaysian Airline System (MAS) added six B747s to its fleet of 20 jets and nine F50s to its fleet of 15 smaller aircraft.

The airports at Kuala Lumpur, Penang, Kota Baharu, Kota Kinabalu, and Kuching are international airports and equipped to handle wide-body aircraft. Airports for domestic flights in Peninsular Malaysia are located in Kuala Trenganu, Kuantan, Alor Star, Ipoh, and Malacca. There are projects under way to upgrade the Langkawi Airport to allow landing for A300 aircraft in order to accommodate the increased tourist traffic, as well as a project to improve the runway at Penang. MAS serves the United States, Japan, India, Australia, the Middle East, the People's Republic of China, as well as four cities in Europe.

INVESTMENT CLIMATE

Taxation and Regulatory Conditions

The Ministry of Finance coordinates the Malaysian government's tax system through the Inland Revenue Department and the Customs and Excise Department. The major public revenues of the government of Malaysia are provided by the following:

- income taxes on companies and individuals
- indirect taxes such as sales tax, service tax, and customs and excise duties
- estate and stamp duties
- real property gains tax

Sources of Income Liable to Taxation

Income taxable in Malaysia includes the following: income obtained from gains or profits from a business; gains or profits from employment; dividends, interest, or discounts; rents, royalties, or premiums, pensions, annuities, or other periodic payments; and any other gains or profit. For residents of Malaysia, both income from Malaysia and income remitted from outside Malaysia are subject to taxation. For nonresidents, only income from Malaysia is taxable. Generally, nonresidents are not subject to tax on income from employment in Malaysia if the period of employment is less than 60 days. There is no tax on capital gains, with the exception of a tax on the gain from real property held less than five years.

FINANCING AND CAPITAL MARKETS

Payment Modalities

The Currency

The Malaysian currency is the ringgit or Malaysian dollar. The external value of the ringgit is based on its relationship to a weighted basket of the currencies of Malaysia's major trading partners, including the United States. The ringgit exchange rate in terms of the U.S. dollar, the intervention currency, is determined in the foreign exchange market. Bank Negara, Malaysia's Central Bank, intervenes in order to promote relative stability in the value of the ringgit in relation to the basket of currencies. Rates for all other currencies are determined on the basis of the Malaysian dollar versus U.S. dollar rate and the U.S. dollar rates for those currencies in markets abroad.

LICENSING, PATENTS, AND TRADEMARKS

Trademark, Patent, and Copyright Protection

Infringements of intellectual property rights in Malaysia are prevalent but to a lesser degree than in many other Asian countries. Since the early 1980s, the government has enacted a series of laws that have greatly strengthened protection for intellectual property in Malaysia. Although Malaysia is a member of the World Intellectual Property Organization, it has not yet joined the Berne Convention or the Universal Copyright Convention. The Malaysian government understands the importance of intellectual property protection for encouraging foreign investment as well as protecting local producers.

Copyrights

Malaysia passed a new copyright law in 1987 that strengthens protection and explicitly extends coverage to computer software. The law took effect in December 1987 and has already significantly reduced audio and computer software piracy. Malaysia does not yet provide adequate protection to foreign works but has presented its documents in order to accede to the Berne Convention.

Patents

Malaysia passed a new patent law in 1983 and implemented it in 1986. The law has strong penalties for violators and sound implementing procedures; however, the registration and technical review offices are backlogged. The United States has provided technical assistance and training in the United States and Malaysia to help the government set up its own patent system. The new law and its strong administrative support have ended any major problems with pirated pharmaceutical products. Patents registered in Malaysia generally have a duration of 15 years and may have longer duration under certain circumstances. A person who has neither his or her domicile nor his or her residence in Malaysia must use a local patent agent to proceed before the Patent Registration Office or to institute suit.

Trademarks

Any person who registers or applies for protection of a trademark in a foreign country designated by the Malaysian government is entitled to registration of that trademark in Malaysia, provided that application for registration is made within six months from the date of registration in the foreign country concerned.

VISITING AND LOCATING

General Travel Checklist

Visas

Passports are required for all visitors to Malaysia. Visas are not required for purposes of business, tourism, transit, or social visit for a stay of less than three months. Those desiring clearance for stays of longer duration of those seeking employment, education, or research should consult the Embassy of Malaysia in Washington, D.C. Visitors staying for more than one year are required to obtain a national registration card.

Currency

The currency used in Malaysia is the Malaysian ringgit.

Getting Around

Taxis and buses are abundant and inexpensive in all of the major cities.

Accommodations and Housing

Kuala Lumpur is host to a number of first-class hotels that compare favorably with first-class hotels in major European and American cities. Most hotels in Kuala Lumpur have fitness centers.

Electricity Supply

The voltage is 230 volts AC, 50 hertz. Some hotels have 100 volt outlets. Adapters are readily available at hotels.

Business Hours

Government offices and most businesses have hours of 8:00 a.m. to 12:45 p.m. and 2:00 p.m. to 4:15 p.m. from Monday through Thursday. On Friday, hours are generally 8:00 a.m. to 12:15 p.m. and 2:00 p.m. to 4:15 p.m. Saturday hours are from 8:00 a.m. to 12:45 p.m.

Tipping

Tipping is not customary. It is discouraged at the airport and in hotels and restaurants which levy a 10% service charge.

What to Wear

Light summer clothing is best for Malaysia's tropical climate. Dress is usually informal, although on some occasions a jacket and tie may be required for men. Visitors are advised to pack an umbrella when traveling, especially during the monsoon months from November to February.

Health Care

Hospitals and doctors in Kuala Lumpur and other major cities are good. Water is safe to drink, except in some of the more remote rural areas and small towns.

The Media

Malaysia has two television stations that broadcast in Malay, Chinese, Hindi, and English. It also has newspapers that publish in the same languages.

Availability of Foreign Products

Most foreign goods are widely available in the major cities but are significantly more expensive than comparable, locally-produced products.

Shopping

There are numerous shopping centers in Kuala Lumpur and other major cities where everything from clothing to electronics is available.

Dining Out

Kuala Lumpur has a wide variety of restaurants to choose from, ranging from gourmet European cuisine to sidewalk stalls.

Entertainment

There are numerous movie theaters in the major cities, and cabaret shows are frequent in the major hotels, but beyond that, there is little nightlife.

Sightseeing and Tourist Information

In the major cities there are historical buildings and museums and galleries worth visiting, especially in the former colonial trading port of Malacca. The beaches on Malaysia's east coast are stunning and relatively undeveloped in places like Trenganu.

The Expatriate

Immigration and Work Permits

Visas are not required for purposes of business, tourism, transit, or social visits for a stay of less than three months. Those desiring clearance for stays of longer duration or those seeking employment, education, or conducting research should consult the Embassy of Malaysia in Washington, D.C. Visitors staying for more than one year are required to obtain a national registration card.

The Labor Force

Employment and labor relations. Malaysia has 16.9 million people of mixed Malay, Chinese, and Indian background. The population is growing at an annual rate of 2.4%. Malaysia's population density is low compared with other countries in Southeast Asia.

The labor force is growing approximately 2.8% per year and is projected to exceed 6.4 million in 1989. Total employment by the end of 1988 was estimated at 6.1 million. Employment is greatest in the agricultural, mining, and manufacturing sectors; the manufacturing sector is by far the largest employment growth area with annual growth running at 10%. Unemployment has been running between 7% and 8% since 1985 and is concentrated among people in the 15 to 24 year-old age group.

One of the major economic goals set forth under the New Economic Plan is to eliminate the identification of race with economic function. To implement this policy, companies are given goals for employing bumiputras that they are expected to reach over several years. This policy has been generally successful. There are now many more Malays in manufacturing, services, retail trade, and other professions.

Conditions of work. Wages in Malaysia are well below levels prevailing in industrialized countries, but substantially higher than any of its neighbors except Singapore. There is no national minimum wage. Minimum wage legislation covers only certain classes of employees: retail clerks, hotel and restaurant employees, cinema workers, and stevedores not employed directly by a port authority. Minimum monthly wages for these workers are in the US $70 to US $90 range in urban areas and are 10% to 15% lower for rural areas. The effective minimum wage for unskilled labor in the Kuala Lumpur-Petaling Jaya area is M $250 (US $86) per month. In the retail sector, wages below M $250 (US $95) per month are very rare. Average wages for semiskilled production workers are M $600 to M $700 (US $228 to US $267) per month, with many skilled workers making more than M $1,000 ($380) per month.

Three government programs protect Malaysian workers against loss of income because of sickness, injury, death, or old age. There is no welfare program or unemployment compensation in Malaysia, although employers are required by law to pay employees termination benefits.

MALAYSIA

KEY CONTACTS

American Embassy Contacts

American Embassy Kuala Lumpur
376 Jalan Tun Razak
50400 Kuala Lumpur
PO Box 10035
50700 Kuala Lumpur
    Tel: 6/03-248-9011
    Telex: FCSKL MA 32956
    Fax: 60/3-243-5207

Ambassador:	Paul M. Cleveland
Charge d'Affaires:	Thomas C. Jubbard
Political Section:	Thomas P. Hamilton
Economic Section:	Paul H. Blakeburn
Commercial Section:	Paul Walters
Consul (Consular Section):	Allen S.H. Kong
Labor Officer:	Gail Scott (resident of Jakarta)
Administrative Section:	Patrick R. Hayes
Regional Security Officer:	John P. Chornyak
Agricultural Section:	Jeffrey A. Hesse
Public Affairs Officer:	James C. Pollock
Office of the Defense Attache:	Col. George P. McQuillen, U.S.A.

Business Contacts

Consulate-General of Malaysia (Commercial)
630 Third Avenue, 11th Floor
New York, NY 10017
    Tel: 212/682-0232/3
    Telex: TRAEMB 429720

Embassy of Malaysia (Commercial Section)
240 Massachusetts Avenue, NW
Washington, DC 20008
    Telex: 64135 MALAYEM

Consulate General of Malaysia
World Trade Centre Building
350 South Figueroa Street
Los Angeles, CA 90071
   Tel: 213/6171000
   Telex: 4720504 MALA UI

Malaysian Industrial Development Authority

Chicago:
John Hancock Centre, Suite 3350
875 North Michigan Avenue
Chicago, IL 60611
   Tel: 312/787-4532
   Telex: 4330368 MIDA UI

Director-General
3d-6th Floor, Wisma Damansara
Jalan Semantan
PO Box 10618
50720 Kuala Lumpur
Malaysia

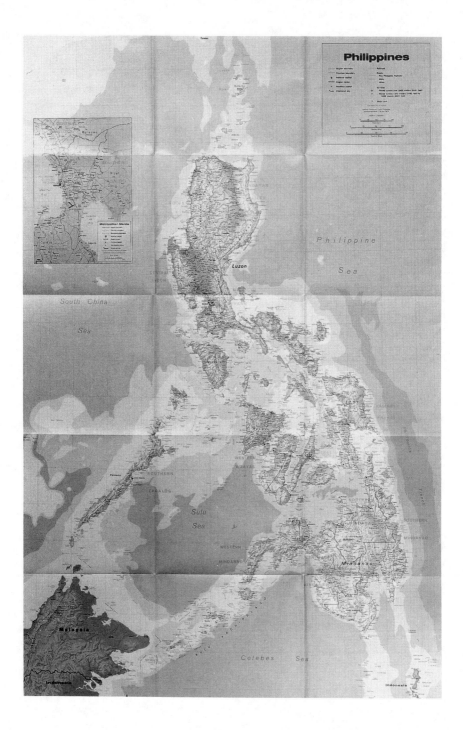

PHILIPPINES

PHILIPPINES

In a Nutshell

		Urban Population
Population (1992)	62,300,000	41.0%

Main Urban Areas		Percentage of Total
Manila	1,728,400	2.7
Quezon City	1,326,000	2.1
Cebu	552,200	0.8

Land Area   115,830 square miles
300,000 square kilometers

Comparable European State   Slightly smaller than Italy
Comparable U.S. State   Slightly larger than Arizona

Language   Filipino and English

Common Business Language   English

Currency   Philippine peso (1P = 100 centavos)

Best Air Connection   San Francisco-Seoul-Manila
(Mon., Tues., Wed., Fri., Sat.)
United Airlines 800/538-2929

Los Angeles - Honolulu-Guam-
Manila (Tues., Wed., Thurs., Sun.)
Continental Air 800/231-0856

Best Hotel   Hyatt Regency
($143/night as of 2/92)

CHAPTER CONTENTS

INTRODUCTION AND REGIONAL ORIENTATION

Geographical and Historical Background

The Philippines consists of 7,100 islands, 11 of which occupy 95% of the land area. Ninety-five percent of the population lives on these 11 larger islands.

Politically, the Philippines is divided into 12 regions and 74 provinces. Internal politics and social stability have been the source of great problems for many years, due in part to a lack of economic equity between inhabitants of the rural and urban areas.

The country does not look like a promising business opportunity for the near future (1992-1995). It is impossible to assure investors that the economy can rebound from the political crises; nor can it be guaranteed that political problems will not disrupt the economy.

POLITICAL/INSTITUTIONAL INFRASTRUCTURE

Geographically detached, the islands that make up the Philippines create a big challenge to political organization. Since 1898 to 1946, it has relied on the United States for economic and political development. The leaders since have, for the most part, worked concurrently with the United States government since 1946.

The United States is the Philippines largest trading partner, followed by Japan and Europe. During 1989, U.S. exports and imports amounted to US $2.2 billion and US $3.1 billion respectively. The problems in the Philippines, however, are beyond the United States' control. Political instability continues to plague the Philippines. President Corazon Aquino's popularity is sagging. Most Filipinos are frustrated with her inability to end corruption and inflation. On top of this is the lack of support from the armed forces. Currently, President Aquino must work with the military to maintain power. The failed December 1989 coup attempt underscored the deep divisions within the military and the opportunism of some politicians. If the president is going to renew stability, she must work with the opposition to prevent further challenges to her power. More is at stake this time because foreign investment is a prominent factor in the Philippine economy.

In January 1992, the U.S. Department of State issued a travel advisory concerning the Philippines, urging caution for Americans. The State Department reported several kidnappings of resident and nonresident U.S. citizens. Security threats are expected to continue as the United States withdraws its forces from Subic Naval Base. Luzon should be avoided because of the presence of the New People's

Army and armed bandits. Visayas and Mindanao are also unsafe because of crime and insurgencies.

INVESTMENT CLIMATE

The Philippine economy remains the most problematic in the Pacific Rim, primarily because of political instability. President Aquino has helped improve the investment climate since the fall of Ferdinand Marcos, especially by investing in the infrastructure projects and privatizing state-owned enterprises. However, many obstacles still remain, including the inefficient bureaucratic delays and lack of governmental responsiveness.

Manila may loosen investment rules soon in order to mitigate the impact of perceived political risk. Exporting to the Philippines is much easier now because nearly all import licensing requirements are eliminated. In January 1990, duties on public transportation equipment, medicine, and chemicals were temporarily reduced by 10%, providing more incentives. However, few investors will finalize investments in the Philippines until the political situation stabilizes - which is not likely to happen in the immediate future. In 1989, GNP grew in the Philippines 5.6%. Consumption growth continued in 1989 but at a slower rate than in the previous two years. Gross domestic product growth was 5.6% in 1989.

The coup attempt changed all positive trends of 1989. GDP slowed in 1990 due to poor low productivity. Labor unions have been militant as inflation eroded the gains of the 40% minimum wage hike in 1989. The 11% inflation rate for 1989 rapidly increased in 1990. Inflation will cause consumption to decline; therefore, the economic growth depends on investment. In addition, the Philippine peso depreciated 8.6% in the first months of 1990 and probably will continue to slide at this rate.

High interest rates and political uncertainty indicate that investment growth will also slow. To add to this, new taxes have been imposed as a part of the IMF-requested austerity plan to fight the budget deficit. All of this will increase the current account deficit and cause protracted economic problems.

Due to these rapidly increasing economic and political problems, nearly 50,000 Filipinos emigrate each year. The Philippines has one of the most highly educated citizenries in Southeast Asia. However, the steady supply of the well-educated college graduates are decreasing due to emigration. As a result, there are fewer highly trained personnel for managerial and technical positions.

Other problems include frequent power shortages, rocketing inflation, high borrowing costs, and the government's failure to complete government projects.

FUTURE PROSPECTS

Established multinational corporations may be winners in the Philippines as the Philippine Congress introduces its privatization programs to create openings for new acquisitions. Major infrastructural programs currently in progress should improve the operating environment. However, the market for new investors is very risky.

Investment opportunities are in industries using the Philippines' labor and natural resources. These include electronics, software development, agribusiness, aquaculture, and light manufacturing of products such as soft toys, Christmas ornaments, and high-quality ceramics.

PHILIPPINES

KEY CONTACTS

American Embassy Contacts

American Embassy Manila
1201 Roxas Blvd.
APO San Francisco 96528
   Tel: 63/2-521-7116
   Telex: 722-27366 AME PH

Commercial Office
395 Buendia Avenue
Extension Makati
   Tel: 63/2-818-6674
   Telex: 22708 COSEC PH

Ambassador:	Frank G. Wisner
Deputy Chief of Mission:	Kenneth M. Quinn
Political Section:	John D. Finney, Jr.
Economic Section:	John P. Modderno
Commercial Section:	Theodore J. Villinski
Administrative Section:	Robert A. MacCallum
Consul (Consular Section):	Bruce A. Beardsley
Labor Officer:	James P. Dodd
Immigration and Naturalization Services:	Gregory Smith
Regional Security Officer:	Philip E. Jornlin
Agricultural Section:	Lyle Moe
Agency for International Development:	Malcolm H. Butler
Public Affairs Officer:	Robert F. Jordan
Office of the Defense Attache:	Col. Terry C. Isaacson, U.S.A.F.
Joint U.S. Military Advisory Group:	Mg. Thomas H. Harvey, Jr., U.S.A.
Internal Revenue Service:	Marilyn Dearsman

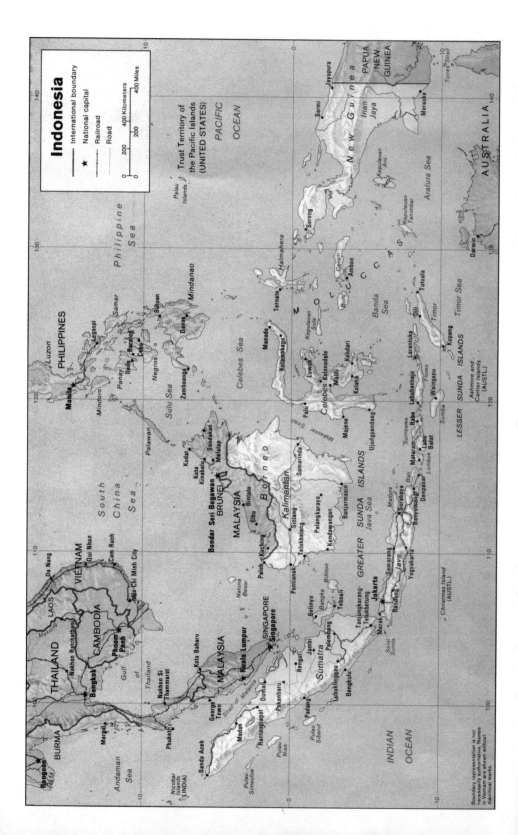

SINGAPORE

SINGAPORE
In a Nutshell

		Urban Population
Population (1992)	2,800,000	100%
Main Urban Areas		Percentage of Total
Singapore	2,600,000	92.8

Land Area	220 square miles
	570 square kilometers
Comparable European State	Slightly less than four times the size of Liechtenstein
Comparable U.S. State	Slightly less than four times the size of Washington, D.C.
Language	Chinese, Malay, Tamil, English
Common Business Language	English
Currency	Singapore dollar (1S$ = 100 cents)
Best Air Connection	Los Angeles-Tokyo-Singapore (daily) San Francisco-Hong Kong-Singapore (daily) Singapore Air 800/472-3333
Best Hotel	Hyatt Regency ($257/night as of 2/92)

CHAPTER CONTENTS

INTRODUCTION AND REGIONAL ORIENTATION

Geographical and Historical Background

Located at the crossroads of Asia, the island state of Singapore is a major international port and an excellent site for a regional marketing, warehouse, and distribution base. The primary marketing regions consist of Indonesia, Malaysia, and Brunei, but many firms also cover Thailand, India, and the Philippines. Excellent transportation and communications infrastructure allow firms to expand their market regions even further if desired.

There are virtually no barriers to trade in services. Capital goods are imported duty free with only a few exceptions; duties are imposed only to reflect social, religious, or cultural values, not to protect local industries. This is due to the fact that Singapore depends on foreign trade and investment for economic growth. In fact, the government of Singapore provides many incentives to foreign investors. Since 1985 it has deregulated sectors of the economy and lowered personal and business taxes to encourage foreign investment.

The main problems facing the Singapore market are rising inflation due to rising import costs and labor costs, chronic labor shortages, an insufficient educational system to match its growing prosperity, and overpopulation resulting in social unrest. One dilemma associated with Singapore's economic growth is its removal from the United States' Generalized System of Preferences scheme. While the actual economic loss will not be serious, the implications of Singapore's status as a developed country give more cause for anxiety. Not only will Singapore lose the privileges and concessions accorded to a developing country, but it will also have to be a full-paying member of all international bodies.

However, the government actively works to improve the economic environment, especially to encourage investment. The current labor shortage has prompted the government's interest in capital-intensive investments. Industries such as high-tech, information technology, and automotive sectors are highly promoted. In all, its large foreign exchange market, healthy banking industry, location as the regional hub, and attractive investment climate make Singapore a promising business opportunity.

Political Overview

Singapore gained formal independence from its status as a British colony in 1965. Its excellent location to the South China Sea and the Indian Ocean has made it an important naval base and commercial port for 175 years. The capital city and location for 95% of the population, Singapore has an appearance of modern progress which disguises the deep Asian culture and tradition.

Singapore's consistent political leadership contributes to the enduring culture. Since June 1959, when Singapore was nominally self-governing, the island has been governed by the same Prime Minister, Lee Kwan Yew. In 1989, he announced as his successor a deputy prime minister, Goh Chok Tong; however, he has not as yet abrogated his power. U.S. sources expect him to step down some time this year, although the new leadership does not promise any dramatic changes. Goh Chok Tong is expected to follow the rule of Lee Kuan Yew.

While the prime minister and the ruling political party, the People's Action party, PAP, have maintained cohesion, it also tends to stifle criticism. Radio and television services are state-owned. Newspapers require annual licenses and are widely criticized for a policy of censorship. The concentration of power and patronage in the hands of one group also presents a problem. Seven opposition parties contested the 1980 parliamentary elections, but the ruling party achieved the widest margin, capturing 78% of the votes. Yet widespread support for the opposition in the 1988 parliamentary elections revealed a slight change in PAP's power. It garnered 61%, leaving the other 39% to opposition parties.

Educational inequality also plagues the island. As education becomes a more important determinant of income potential, the wealth gap between the Chinese and Malay populations will widen. This will fuel the ethnic tensions that already exist and create problems for the government, but should not threaten the economic environment.

While the republic was a founding member of the Association of Southeast Asian Nations (ASEAN) formed in 1967 along with Malaysia, Thailand, Indonesia, and the Philippines (and joined in 1984 by Brunei), at first it was only nominally interested in regional cooperation. By 1976, Singapore had gained more autonomy from the UK, thus permitting it to draw closer to its neighbors. It has supported the idea of regional solidarity, occasionally facing problems due to the military interests of the United States and former Soviet Union.

Singapore faces its own political uncertainties; it is a young country that has been ruled by the same prime minister since its independence in 1965. Nevertheless, Singapore remains one of the world's most politically stable countries, and its population enjoys a high standard of living. The financial industry sees the political institutions as ultra-stable. For the most part they can live with a controlled press, but cannot live with exchange and financial control. Since all stand to benefit, this situation is likely to continue.

Economic Outlook

Singapore seriously emphasizes development to compete with the major markets in the world. The country is reaping the dividends of the austerity program the government imposed in 1985 to restore its competitiveness. Having completely overcome the effects of the country's 1985-1986 recession, the economy showed impressive growth of 8.8% in 1987 and 11.0% in 1988. External demand was the overwhelming factor in the outstanding economic expansion, accounting for nine-tenths of the growth. Total exports rose 29%, primarily in the non-oil sector. Disk drives, integrated circuits, and data processing machines led the way, while exports of consumer electronics products and chemicals were also impressive.

Singapore is the computer disk-drive capital of the world, producing roughly 90% of the world's supply. Seagate Technology (USA) is the country's single-largest employer, with a workforce of 12,400. Seagate has recently expanded its manufacturing and assembly operations into Thailand.

The basic economic thrust of the government is to reorient its manufacturing sector toward more capital-intensive, higher value-added industries and promote services and Singapore's position as a potential regional hub. The government has identified the financial sector as key to the development of regional services base, along with those industries that capitalize on the country's strategic location: transportation, communications, and tourism. It is also seeking to diversify its export markets.

Singapore's major trading partners include Japan, Malaysia, Hong Kong, Taiwan, and Thailand. Singapore's trade with Indonesia is believed to be substantial but, by mutual agreement, their bilateral trade statistics are not published. Its total trade with China has been increasing an average of 19% over the last six years.

Due to labor shortages and high profits, labor costs are rising. At the same time, productivity growth is slowing, especially in manufacturing.

The labor shortage has become very serious at all skill levels, but it is especially acute for workers with technical qualifications. The government has responded with tailored retraining and skills development programs and by allowing employers to import foreign labor, but its response cannot keep up with the demand. Fearing social problems from an over-dependence on low-wage foreign workers, the government recently imposed limits on their numbers and sharply increased the cost of employing them. Acknowledging that lack of labor availability, it hopes companies will upgrade production technology to reduce their labor needs. However, experience shows that the sort of labor to capital intensive restructuring the government is promoting does not so much reduce demand for labor as it shifts the needed employee qualifications to a higher level. This will assure a continuing strong demand for a better educated workforce.

The tight labor market has been eased by foreign workers imported from Malaysia, Indonesia, Thailand, the Philippines, India, and Sri Lanka. Demand for foreign workers is more acute in the industrial and construction sectors. However, in response to social and political considerations, the government plans to eliminate the need for unskilled foreign workers by 1992.

The Singapore government has made a conscious effort to reduce its role in the economy and to allow more room for the private sector. Accordingly, the government has used its favorable fiscal situation to reduce tax rates and promote investment through tax incentives. Singapore has many incentives for attracting direct foreign investment. There are no formal screening mechanisms to permit certain investments and exclude others; however, it uses incentives to promote specific industries consistent with its overall development strategy.

In addition, Singapore has signed investment-guarantee agreements with several countries including: Canada, France, West Germany, the Netherlands, Switzerland, United Kingdom, United States, Belgo-Luxembourg Economic Union, and Sri Lanka. Under these agreements, investments by nations or companies of both contracting parties in each other's respective country are protected for a specific period, usually 15 years, against war and noncommercial risks of expropriation. In the event of noncommercial risks, Singapore will compensate the foreign investors either directly or through their governments. Generally, the compensation will be based on the market value of the property destroyed or confiscated.

Another positive aspect of doing business in Singapore is the superb organization and infrastructure. Situated at a crossroad of international shipping and air routes, Singapore is a center for transportation in Southeast Asia. The transportation network features state-of-the-art technology and continues to be improved and expanded. The Port of Singapore is the second largest cargo-handling port in the world, consisting of five gateways with a new container port planned for completion in 1992. The island is linked to Malaysia and Thailand by highway and by the Malaysian Railway System. The republic possesses a modern network of roads and expressways spanning 2,758 kilometers. In addition, Singapore has a mass rapid transport subway system covering 27 kilometers.

Telecommunications facilities are modern and comprehensive with worldwide air, sea, and telecommunications links. Singapore Telecom makes continuous efforts to upgrade and expand its national and international telecommunications system and has budgeted US $900 million from 1988-1992 on an improvement program. It is currently liberalizing its policies, especially regarding international value-added networks, and encourages joint ventures and research and development projects.

Demographics

Socioeconomic Indicators and Conditions

Singapore maintains a free and open market policy. As a regional trading, sales, service, and warehousing center, it continues to import more than twice as much from the United States as the other countries of the Association of Southeast Asian Nations. The United States is Singapore's major trading partner and a major foreign investor. U.S. exports to Singapore totaled $5.7 billion in 1988, an increase of 42% over 1987. U.S. imports from Singapore in 1988 were $8.2 billion, up from $6.4 billion in 1987.

Despite earlier warnings about slower trade growth, the latest information from the government of Singapore indicates that its trade in 1990 was not adversely affected by the Gulf crisis or the U.S. recession. The government announced that the gross domestic product grew by 8.3% in 1990. Productivity growth rose from 4.6% to 4.8% from 1988 to 1989 and hit an impressive 5.6% for the first quarter of 1990. Total economic growth fell to under 6% in 1991, based on Singapore's perception of the effects of a recession in the United States.

Singapore hopes that increasing trade with Southeast Asia will offset the negative effects of a U.S. recession. The republic believes that the economies of the region are still strong enough to lessen the impact of the worldwide slowdown and will help to diminish Singapore's dependence on the U.S. market. The strong growth in U.S. exports to Singapore has slowed the growth of perennial trade surplus that Singapore has enjoyed since 1984. Barring any further economic downturn in world demand, it is projected that U.S. exports to Singapore should surpass the 1990 level of $8.02 billion to reach $9.3 billion in 1991.

Singapore is a financial center for much of Asia. Its financial industry was developed to support trading but has expanded to include the full range of banking services. Combining these services with the country's central geographic location, high credit standing, and excellent communications facilities, makes Singapore attractive for U.S. exporters. In addition, Singapore is an ideal base for penetrating the Asian market due to the virtual absence of governmental and commercial corruption, its business orientation, and increasing preferences for U.S. products and services.

Finance and Investment Policies

The goal of the government's finance and investment policy is to make the country as attractive as possible to foreign investors. In most cases, Singapore does not distinguish between foreign private investment and local investment. However, foreign investment is restricted in certain areas, including insurance, banking, and related financial services.

The Singapore government stresses the promotion of the information technology industry, and the market has become quite sophisticated. Both the government — Singapore's largest buyer of information technology — and the private sector are highly receptive to new firms offering quality products and services.

Manufacturing firms interested in operating in Singapore usually negotiate incentives with the Economic Development Board (EDB), a statutory board operating under the guidance of the Ministry of Trade and Industry. The EDB administers most of the investment incentives offered by the government and approves investment based on the sophistication of the product and the technology the firm proposes to bring with it. A premium is placed on maximizing the capital/labor ratio and the value-added per worker in any advanced manufacturing proposed. Companies proposing to use the most advanced manufacturing technology available are favored by the EDB. Relatively labor-intensive assembly operations are generally not offered incentives and may not be approved.

Recently, the Singapore government, in a bid to bring more high-tech industry to the country, announced plans to invest its own money in joint ventures with multinationals. In the first deal, the EDB has taken a stake in a four-way, US $300 million joint venture involving Texas Instruments Corporation, Canon, and Hewlett-Packard to build a wafer-fabrication facility to manufacture advanced four and 16 megabyte dynamic random access memory chips in Singapore.

Policies to Attract New Business

Investment Incentives and Privileges

Singapore offers a number of incentives for foreign private investment:

Pioneer status. Under this exemption, profits of manufacturing and certain service companies may be exempted by the Minister for Finance for a period of five to 10 years.

Expansion incentive. The profits from approved plant expansion (over S $10 million) in productive equipment and machinery are exempted from corporate tax up to five years.

Export incentive. This exemption provides for a 90% reduction in corporate tax (from 33% to 4%) on export profits. The tax relief period is an additional three years for companies receiving pioneer status and five years for nonpioneer companies.

Investment allowance. Companies starting up or increasing the manufacture of any product can apply for a tax exemption worth up to 50% of the fixed capital expenditure on specified items.

International consulting incentive. This incentive is extended to companies engaged in technical advisory services, design and engineering fabrication of equipment, and management and supervision of installation construction and data processing. These services must be for overseas projects, and only companies earning more than S $1 million per year from such services are eligible. The incentive is a concessionary 20% corporate tax rate for a period of five years.

Foreign loans for productive equipment. The 40% withholding tax on interest payable to foreign lenders for loans can be exempted if the foreign loan is no less than S $200,000 and is made for the purchase of productive equipment for manufacturing and related activities. Any productive equipment financed with an approved foreign loan cannot be sold or otherwise disposed of before the loan has been repaid in full without the prior consent of the Minister for Finance.

Accelerated depreciation allowances. Capital expenditures on robots, computers, and other prescribed office automation equipment are eligible for a 100% write-off in the first year. Industrial enterprises may claim an accelerated allowance of 33-1/3% per annum for a period of three years on capital expenditure incurred on plant machinery.

Research and development (R&D) incentives. Various incentives are offered to manufacturing companies engaging in R&D and to specialized R&D institutions servicing manufacturing companies. Some of these include the following:

- Manufacturing companies that include R&D as a part of their operations may be considered for an additional year or more of pioneer status.
- In addition to the normal capital allowance, an investment allowance of up to 50% of the fixed investment in R&D equipment can be considered.
- Heavy recurrent expenses (subject to a maximum to be determined by the Minister for Finance) for manpower, materials, and utilities for R&D activities may be considered for double tax deduction. This relief is available for up to five years.
- Payments for approved know-how, patent rights, and manufacturing licenses can be capitalized and written-off over a five-year period.
- Plant and machinery used for R&D can be depreciated over three years.
- R&D buildings (like industrial buildings) can be depreciated over 25 years.

- Exemptions of 50% to 100% from withholding taxes may be claimed on payments to foreigners of royalties, technical assistance fees, or contributions to R&D.

Offshore income. Financial institutions may apply for a concessionary corporate tax rate of 10% (versus 33%) on offshore income derived from operations of Asian currency units. This concessionary tax rate is also provided to member firms on the Singapore International Monetary Exchange (SIMEX) on income derived from transactions in gold bullion or in approved commodity or financial future contracts on any approved exchange or in any approved market.

Free Trade Zones/Special Economic Zones

The free trade zones came into operation in 1969 providing a range of facilities and services for the storage and re-export of dutiable and controlled goods. There are six free trade zones — five for seaborne cargoes (PSA gateways and Jurong Port) and one for air cargoes (Changi Airport).

Goods are stored within the zones without any customs documentation until they are released in the market. They can also be processed and re-exported with minimal customs formalities.

APPROACHING THE MARKET

State and Private Services

Market Research

Recognized as an essential and effective marketing tool, market research is being utilized with increasing frequency in Singapore with very satisfactory results. Several firms have been established to supply this service and have developed an acceptable competence in professional market research. These firms are constantly expanding their activities to meet the growing demand for their expertise.

Although professional market investigation services are available, many local trading firms conduct market inquires on an ad hoc basis. While the results are often good, they vary according to the competence of the firms and their staff responsible for market planning and development. Foreign suppliers having agency contacts with local firms are able to obtain the most useful market assessments and market development guidance from their agents.

Setting Up Business Operations

Forms of Business Organization

Limited liability company. A limited liability company is the most common form of business entity in Singapore. The company, either private or public, may be limited by shares or a guarantee. Formation procedures for a private company include the following:

1. Advise the Registrar of Companies of the proposed name and obtain written approval for its use.

2. If the proposed company has foreign participation, and is a trading company or shipping company, the Registrar will obtain the approval of the Trade Development Board before registering the company. In the case of a manufacturing company or finance company, the respective approval of the Economic Development Board and the Monetary Authority of Singapore should be obtained by the applicant.

3. Two or more persons should subscribe their names to the memorandum and articles of association of the proposed company.

4. An application is submitted to the Registrar of Companies enclosing a copy of the company's memorandum and articles of association together with a statutory declaration of compliance with the Companies Act and a certification of identity.

5. A certificate of incorporation is issued, and from the date of the issue, the company may commence business.

Fees for registration of companies, payable on incorporation, are calculated on a sliding scale determined by the company's authorized share capital. They are contained in the Second Schedule to the Companies Act.

Branches of foreign corporations. A branch of a foreign corporation must submit the following to the Registrar of Companies within one month after it commences operations in Singapore:

- a copy of the corporation's certificate of incorporation;
- a copy of its charter statutes or memorandum and articles of association;
- a list of its directors and a list of its local directors (if applicable);

- a memorandum of appointment stating the names and addresses of two agents in Singapore, together with a statutory declaration verifying this memorandum;
- a statutory declaration by the agents; and
- a notice of the situation of its registered office in Singapore.

The corporation is required to forward a copy of its annual accounts and its audited Singapore branch accounts to the Registrar of Companies within two months after its annual general meeting in its country of incorporation.

Sole traders and partnerships.   Most businesses can be carried on in the form of a sole trader or a partnership. All sole traders and partnerships, as well as changes to partnership personnel, must be registered under the Business Registration Act of 1973.

An ordinary partnership occurs when the partners are jointly liable for the debts and obligations of the partnership. A limited partnership is a partnership where one or more partners may enjoy limited liability to the extent of their capital contributions. A limited partnership must have one or more general partners to be liable without limit for the debts of the firm.

Representative offices.   A representative office is usually staffed by internationally assigned personnel and is assisted by a small number of locally employed personnel. The office will be established by a non-Singapore company and its functions include the following:

- acting as a liaison with sales agents and customers in Singapore and other countries;
- soliciting orders for products or services;
- providing market intelligence to the head office;
- advising purchases on the optimum use of products or services; and
- promoting market awareness of products and services and assisting in the planning of advertising and promotional activities.

A representative office, however, cannot engage in business, conclude contracts, or open or negotiate any letters of credit. Therefore, it has no exposure to Singapore income tax.

Procedural approval must be obtained from the Trade Development Board for setting up a representative office. It normally takes about two weeks for the board to process the application.

Sales Promotion, Fairs, Conferences, and Advertising

Advertising is widely used in Singapore and most forms of advertising familiar to the exporter are available. There are several advertising and public relations firms that provide the exporting company or its agent with the complete range of public relations services.

The most effective media advertising is found in the daily newspapers (circulation 800,000 in the four official languages). Most of the Singapore business and consumer public can be reached in the English language press.

Rising family incomes make radio and television a very popular medium for advertising. Over 70% of the population listens daily to Singapore Broadcasting Corporation (SBC) radio broadcasts. SBC's television network operates 155 hours weekly on three separate channels, offering a full range of programs in color. Both radio and television offer substantial commercial time and program sponsorships. U.S. consumer, news, and trade journals have a wide circulation, particularly among the more affluent international business and professional customers, many of whom are headquartered in Singapore.

Transportation and Freight (Air/Sea)

Situated at a crossroads of international shipping and air routes, Singapore is a center for transportation in Southeast Asia. The transportation network features state-of-the-art technology and continues to be improved and expanded. In 1982, an international airport was built at Changi, and a second passenger terminal is nearing completion. Singapore is served by more than 40 international airlines in addition to its own national carrier connecting most major cities.

The Port of Singapore is the second largest cargo-handling port in the world. Five gateways comprise the Port of Singapore (PSA): Keppel Wharves, Tanjong Pagar Container Terminal, Jurong Port, Pasir Panjang Wharves, and Sembawang Wharves.

In 1987, the total volume of seaborne cargo handled at Singapore's wharves, anchorages, oil refineries, and other privately operated bulk-storage terminals increased by 4.8%. The combined cargo throughout amounted to 118.3 million freight tons. This improved performance was largely due to an increase in containerized cargo attributed to economic growth. A new container port featuring state-of-the-art material handling facilities is planned for completion in 1992.

INVESTMENT CLIMATE

Taxation and Regulatory Conditions

Sources of Income Liable to Taxation

All gains or profits from any trade, business, profession, or vocation, earnings from employment, dividends, interest and discounts, pensions and annuities; and rents, royalties, and earnings from property can be taxed.

Company Tax

Corporations pay a flat tax of 33% after deductions for certain expenses, depreciation allowances, trading losses, and donations to approved charities.

Deductions are allowed for all direct and overhead expenses incurred in generating income. The list of allowable deductions includes, but is not limited to, the following items: interest on loans, dividends declared, rent, expenses incurred for repair of premises, plant, machinery or fixtures, bad debts, contributions to approved pensions, and building, machinery, and equipment depreciation.

Personal Income Tax

Personal income tax for temporary residents, short-term visiting employees, non-residents, and residents are explained below.

Temporary residents. Income temporary residents of Singapore receive from sources outside Singapore is exempt from Singapore income tax under certain conditions. The individual must not have resided in Singapore for a period or periods equaling six months in one year. Directors of companies are liable for a flat income tax rate of 30% regardless of the length of their stay in Singapore.

Short-term visiting employees. Income derived from employment in Singapore by nonresident employees who stay in Singapore for not more than 60 days in one year is exempt from Singapore income tax.

Nonresidents. Persons residing in Singapore for more than 60 days, but less than 183 days in one year are normally considered to be nonresidents. The income of such persons (whether paid in Singapore or not) derived from employment in Singapore is taxable at a flat rate of 15%, provided the tax payable is not less than that payable by a resident in the same circumstances. Income from most other sources is taxable at a flat rate of 40%.

Residents. An individual who has resided in Singapore for 183 days or more in one year is considered a resident, and he or she is liable for tax on income derived from or received in Singapore on the same basis as Singapore citizens. Personal income tax is charged on a sliding scale ranging from 4% to 30% after deductions.

Property Tax

Property tax is levied on immovable properties. A flat rate of 23% is levied on all properties other than owner-occupied temporary structures and approved development projects which will continue to enjoy a flat rate of S $6 per annum and 12% respectively. A surcharge of 10% of the annual value of a property is levied on all residential properties. Owners who are Singapore citizens, permanent residents, or companies registered and carrying on business in Singapore are eligible for exemption. If the residential properties are condominium units or apartments in buildings of not less than six stories, eligibility for exemption is opened to all categories of owners. The previous 30% property tax rebate on commercial and industrial properties has been increased to 50%. The additional 20% rebate will be awarded only if it is passed fully to tenants.

FINANCING AND CAPITAL MARKETS

Banking and Other Financial Institutions

Singapore is the major financial center for Southeast Asia. Its financial activities have become an important adjunct to its export-oriented industries and its development as a manufacturing center. As of March 1986, there were 136 banks in Singapore — 37 with full licenses and 85 with offshore licenses. American banks providing full banking services include Citibank, Chase Manhattan, and Bank of America.

The Development Bank of Singapore (DBS), owned by the government and a number of financial institutions, is the major source of medium- and long-term loans in Singapore dollars. Commercial banks, however, are increasingly providing medium- and long-term loans to manufacturing firms. DBS extends credit for five to ten years at competitive interest rates, covering up to 50% of plant and machinery costs and up to 65% of the value of factory buildings. Higher wages are available for particularly desirable projects and for expansion loans.

Several merchant banks have been formed to assist in the financing of Singapore's rapid industrial growth. These banks' activities cover areas not serviced by commercial banks and include capital equipment leasing, medium-term currency loans, direct investment in selected industries, and consulting services from their staffs of lawyers, brokers, and accountants.

Payment Modalities

The Currency

The unit of currency is the Singapore dollar which, is divided into one hundred cents. The Singapore dollar is readily exchangeable at banks and foreign exchange offices.

Financial Market Operations

Money Market

The Singapore foreign exchange market is the second largest in Asia after Tokyo. The major currencies traded, namely the Deutsche mark, yen sterling, Swiss franc, and Australian dollar are usually quoted against the U.S. dollar.

Securities Market

Since May 1987, there has been an active government securities market in taxable book-entry securities, ranging in maturity from three months to five years. Eight market-makers, called primary dealers, ensure liquidity by making two-way prices in all market conditions. Applications for new issues of government securities, offered at regular auctions, are submitted through the primary dealers. In the secondary market, there are 35 secondary dealers among the banks, merchant banks, and stockbroking firms dealing with customers in amounts as small as $1,000 for notes and bonds and $10,000 for Treasury bills.

Futures Market

The Singapore International Money Exchange (SIMEX) commenced trading in futures contracts in Singapore with the introduction of an international gold futures contract with delivery in London on July 5, 1984. Trading on the exchange is on an "open outcry" basis. The financial futures market also features a unique system of mutual offset arrangement between the Chicago Mercantile Exchange in Chicago and SIMEX. Such an arrangement allows contracts opened on one exchange to be closed on the other without additional transactional cost for market participants. The linkage is the first of its kind in the world and greatly facilitates "round-the-clock" trading in futures contracts.

LICENSING, PATENTS, AND TRADEMARKS

Trademark, Patent, and Copyright Protection

Singapore uses the United Kingdom Patents Act for the registration of patents. It only registers and protects patents that have been registered in the United Kingdom. Application for a Singapore patent should be made to the Singapore Registry of Trademarks and Patents within three years from the date of sealing in the United Kingdom. The Singapore patent is valid for the life of the U.K. patent.

The trademark law in Singapore is very similar to the U.K. trademark law. The first user or intended user of a trademark is entitled to its registration. Any person claiming to be the proprietor of a trademark may apply for its registration in the United Kingdom or other country with which Singapore has reciprocal trademark relations and may apply for the trademark in Singapore within six months of the foreign registration and receive thereon the same filing date as the earlier foreign registration. Singapore is not a member of an international convention on trademarks.

Singapore's revised Copyright Act took effect on April 10, 1987. On May 19, 1987, Singapore established full copyright relations with the United States. Under the new act, copyright protection is extended to works by U.S. nationals or works first published in the United States. Protected works include music, video, books, and other publications and computer software.

VISITING AND LOCATING

General Travel Checklist

Visas

Passports are required for all visitors. Visas are not required for visitors holding a valid U.S. passport.

Getting Around

Singapore's subway, the Mass Rapid Transit System, provides quick, clean, and inexpensive transportation to most areas of the city. Buses are frequent and cover the entire citystate. Taxis are abundant, air-conditioned, and relatively inexpensive.

Accommodations and Housing

There are numerous world-class hotels in Singapore comparable in luxury, services, professionalism, and cost to five-star hotels in major U.S. and European cities. Housing in Singapore is expensive and ranges from traditional colonial style bungalows to modern centrally air-conditioned apartments.

Electricity Supply

The voltage is 230 volts AC, 50 hertz. Some hotels have 100 volt outlets. Adapters are readily available at hotels.

Business Hours

Businesses operate on a five and a half-day week, Monday through Saturday. Office hours are generally from 8:30 a.m. or 9:00 a.m. to 1:00 p.m. and from 2:00 p.m. to 5:00 p.m. or 5:30 p.m. However, several foreign firms work 44 hours during a five-day week. The hours observed by the government offices are 9:00 a.m. to 4:30 p.m. during the week and 9:00 a.m. to 1:00 p.m on Saturday.

Tipping

Tipping is not customary. It is discouraged at the airport and in hotels and restaurants which levy a 10% service charge.

What to Wear

Light summer clothing is best for Singapore's tropical climate. Dress is usually informal, although on some occasions a jacket and tie may be required for men. Visitors are advised to pack an umbrella when traveling, especially during the monsoon months from November to February.

The Media

There are three Chinese daily newspapers - one morning daily, *Lian He Zao Bao*, and two evening newspapers, *Lian He Wan Bao* and *Shin Min Daily News*. The three English dailies are *The Straits Times*, *Business Times*, and *The New Paper*, which is an afternoon paper. The other newspapers are *Berita Harain*, a Malay daily newspaper, and *Tamil Murasu*, an Indian daily newspaper.

The Singapore Broadcasting Corporation (SBC) is responsible for the programming of the three television and seven radio stations. Both radio and television broadcast in the four official languages of Singapore, and both include news and entertainment programming.

Availability of Foreign Products

Most foreign products are readily available in Singapore, but at a significantly higher cost than similar, locally produced products.

Shopping

Singapore is a shopper's paradise, and this is especially true for electronic products. Bargains are the rule rather than the exception at all of Singapore's abundant shopping centers.

Dining Out

Singapore provides everything from sidewalk stalls to gourmet dining, with a wide variety of Asian and European cuisine.

Entertainment

Singapore has numerous cinemas showing European and American movies, and musical entertainment ranges from the Singapore National Symphony to cabaret shows to pop concerts.

Sightseeing and Tourist Information

There are several beautiful gardens and parks worth visiting as well as museums, the zoo, and the aquarium.

Recreational Opportunities

Most first-class hotels provide fitness centers featuring modern fitness equipment. In addition, Singapore's numerous parks offer the perfect setting for early morning or early evening jogging.

The Expatriate

Immigration and Work Permits

Foreign nationals must apply for employment passes before entering Singapore to take up employment or to establish a business. Approval or permission is usually granted before entry, then finalized after arrival. Professional visit passes are issued to foreign nationals such as consultants, installation personnel, and entertainers, permitting them to work in Singapore on short-term assignments.

Health Care

Singapore has an adequate number of skilled doctors, surgeons, and dentists, many of whom were trained overseas. There are well-equipped government and private hospitals in Singapore. Noncitizens have to pay for treatment in government hospitals, but the costs are usually cheaper than those charged by private hospitals.

The Labor Force

Employment and labor relations. Employment and labor relations are regulated by law. Terms and conditions of service negotiated between unions and management are embodied in collective agreements which have to be certified by the Industrial Arbitration Court. Guidelines for annual wage adjustments are recommended by the National Wages Council representing government, management, and unions.

Conditions of work. Conditions of work are regulated by Part IV of the Employment Act applying to workmen and other employees whose monthly salary does not exceed S $1,250 per month. It fixes the standard working week at 44 hours, with payment at one and half times the hourly rate of pay for overtime and two times the hourly rate of pay for holidays worked and normal weekdays off. Overtime is limited to 72 hours a month. Retirement benefits may be payable after five years of service. Paid sick leave after one year of service is limited to 14 days, but it would be extended to 60 days with hospitalization in any one year. The act also provides for 11 paid public holidays, seven days annual leave after one year's service, and an additional one day's annual leave for every subsequent 12 months of continuous service with the same employer.

Training. The Economic Development Board's role in manpower training dates back to the early 1970s when Singapore began to move into skills-intensive industries. The first joint industry/government training centers were set up with leading international companies to produce a critical core of skilled precision engineering craftsmen vital to the development of the industry.

In the early 1980s, Singapore entered into the next phase of development and emphasis was placed on promoting technology-intensive and higher value-added industries. To meet the special manpower needs of these emerging activities, the EDB established institutes of technology in cooperation with the governments of Japan, Germany, and France. EDB's manpower development programs focus on four main areas: precision engineering, factory automation, mechanics, and industrial electronics.

SINGAPORE

KEY CONTACTS

American Embassy Contacts

American Embassy Singapore
30 Hill Street
Singapore 0617
FPO San Francisco 96699
  Tel: 65/338-0251
  Telex: RS 42289 AMEMB

Ambassador:	Robert D. Orr
Deputy Chief of Mission:	Kent M. Weidemann
Economic/Political Section:	Thomas H. Martin
Commercial Section:	George Ruffner
Consul (Consular Section):	Joan V. Smith
Labor Officer:	Gail P. Scott (resident in Jakarta)
Regional Security Officer:	John F. Donato
Internal Revenue Service:	Jerome Rosenbaum
Administrative Section:	Robert B. Courtney
Agricultural Trade Office:	Geoffrey W. Wiggin
Political Affairs Officer:	Richard D. Gong
Office of the Defense Attache:	Capt George W. Lundy, Jr., U.S.N.
Immigration and Naturalization Section:	William J. Ring, Jr.

Business Contacts

Singapore Economic Development Board
P.C. Chi, Director, Washington Office
1015, 18th Street, NW #710
Washington, DC 20036
  Tel: 202/223-2571
  Fax: 202/223-2572
  Telex: 4973928 EDB UI

EDB Overseas Offices

Head Office:
250 North Bridge Road, #24-00
Raffles City Tower
Singapore 0617
    Tel: 65/336-2288
    Fax: 65/339-6077
    Telex: RS26233

Boston:
55 Wheeler Street
Cambridge, MA 02138
    Tel: 617/497-9392
    Fax: 617/491-6150

Chicago:
Illinois Centre Two, Suite 2307
233 North Michigan Avenue
Chicago, IL 60601
    Tel: 312/644-3730
    Fax: 312/644-4481

Dallas:
Park Central VII
12750 Merit Drive
Suite 1424, LB38
Dallas, TX 75251
    Tel: 214/450-4540
    Fax: 214/450-4543

Los Angeles:
911 Wilshire Boulevard, Suite 950
Los Angeles, CA 90017
    Tel: 213/624-7647
    Fax: 213/624-4412
    Telex: 4720209 TDB LA

New York:
55 East 59th Street
New York, NY 10022
    Tel: 212/421-2200
    Fax: 212/421-2206

San Francisco:
210 Twin Dolphin Drive
Redwood City, CA 94065
    Tel: 415/591-9102
    Fax: 415/591-1328

Washington, DC:
1015 18th Street, NW #710
Washington, DC 20036
    Tel: 202/223-2571 or 202/223-2570
    Fax: 202/223-2572
    Telex: 4973928 EDB UI

Singapore Trade Development Board

Head Office:
1 Maritime Square #10-40 (Lobby D)
World Trade Centre
Telok Blangah Road
Singapore 0409
    Tel: 2719388
    Fax: 2740770/2782518
    Telex: RS 28617/28170 TRADEV

Los Angeles:
Los Angeles World Trade Centre
Thian Tai Chew, Centre Director
350 South Figueroa Street #909
Los Angeles, CA 90071
    Tel: 213/617-7358/9, 617-7397/8
    Fax: 213/617-7367

New York:
Koh Chye Hock, Centre Director
745 5th Avenue #1601
New York, NY 10151
    Tel: 212/421-2207
    Fax: 212/888-2897

Washington, DC:
Cecilia Khoo, First Secretary (Economics)
Embassy of the Republic of Singapore
1824 R Street, NW
Washington, DC 20009-1691

American Business Council of Singapore
1 Scotts Road #16-06
Shaw Centre
Singapore 0922

British Business Association of Singapore
450/452
Inchcape House
Singapore 0511

Japanese Chamber of Commerce and Industry of Singapore
Shenton Way #12-04
Singapore 0106

Singapore Federation of Chambers of Commerce and Industry
47 Hill Street #03-01
Chinese Chamber of Commerce and Industry Building
Singapore 0617

Singapore International Chamber of Commerce
6 Raffles Quay #05-00
Denmark House
Singapore 0104

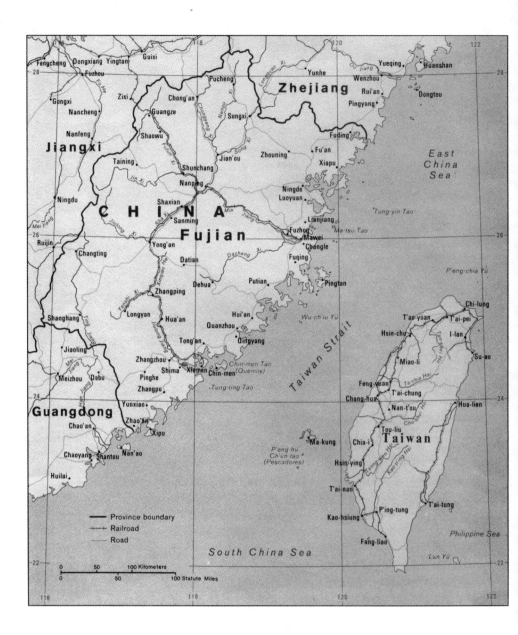

TAIWAN

TAIWAN

In a Nutshell

		Urban Population
Population (1992)	20,500,000	70%

Main Urban Areas		Percentage of Total
Taipei	2,724,829	13.3
Kaohsiung	1,398,667	6.8
Taichung	764,651	3.7
Tainan	685,390	3.3

Land Area	13,895 square miles
	35,988 square kilometers

Comparable European State	Slightly larger than Belgium
Comparable U.S. State	Slightly less than three times the size of Connecticut

Language	Chinese (Mandarin), Taiwanese, and Hakka dialects
Common Business Language	Chinese and English
Currency	New Taiwan dollar (NT$ = 100 cents)
Best Air Connection	Los Angeles-Taipei (daily) San Francisco-Taipei (Tues., Fri., Sun.) New York-Anchorage-Taipei (Mon., Thurs., Sat.) Honolulu-Tokyo-Taipei (daily except Thurs. and Sun.) China Air 800/227-5118
Best Hotel	Grand Hyatt ($276/night as of 2/92)

CHAPTER CONTENTS

INTRODUCTION AND REGIONAL ORIENTATION

Geographical and Historical Background

Taiwan, an island of 35,988 square kilometers, is situated in the Pacific Ocean off the southeastern coast of the Chinese mainland. The Tropic of Cancer bisects the island, which is roughly shaped like a tobacco leaf. Prior to 1949, Taiwan was known as Formosa.

The story of Taiwan's modern-day success begins with the end of World War II. The Japanese, who had occupied the island for 50 years, were departing, and the island was being returned to self-government, calling itself the Republic of China (ROC). The government of the Republic of China instituted a series of economic policies to deal with the economic hardship that ultimately resulted in the creation of an economic miracle in Taiwan. In the early 1950s, the government carried out a land reform program that included generous technical and financial assistance to the agriculture sector. In the early 1960s, export processing zones were established and investment incentives were offered to domestic and foreign investors to promote the exports. In the 1970s, the ROC began to emphasize the strengthening of the island's infrastructure and the development of capital-intensive heavy industries such as steel and petrochemicals. In the 1980s, the government shifted its focus to the promotion of more capital-intensive and higher value-added industries. High-tech industries received special attention and support. At the same time, joint ventures in strategic high-tech industries were encouraged in order to help Taiwan's industrialists gain access to the latest technology from around the world.

Demographics

Socioeconomic Indicators and Conditions

The population of Taiwan exceeded 20.2 million in 1990. With a 1990 per capita GNP of US $ 8,159 and private savings rates consistently higher than 30%, Taiwan's consumers have money on hand and are willing to buy quality products and services. The ratio of income distribution between the richest and poorest groups in society, moreover, stood at only 4.85 to 1, one of the lowest in the world.

Trends in Consumer Demand

With the size of Taiwan families shrinking, more women have joined the work force, greatly enhancing the purchasing power of many households. Foreign exporters with products that can satisfy the sophisticated tastes of this middle class can easily find a niche in the Taiwan market. In 1989, Taiwan's imports rose to a record US $ 52.33 billion, a total that was 5.2% higher than in the previous year and three and a half times that of 1979. Such impressive growth has come primarily as a result of widespread tariff reductions and the appreciation of the New Taiwan (NT) dollar. Taiwan's imports consist mainly of agricultural and industrial raw material, capital goods and consumer items. Imports of consumer goods have experienced vigorous growth.

Political/Institutional Infrastructure

The government is based on a five-power system. The principal organs of the government are as follows:

National Assembly: Composed of elected delegates, their jobs include electing or recalling the president and vice-president, amending the constitution, or voting on constitutional amendments.

The President: The president is elected by the National Assembly for a six-year term and may be re-elected for a second term.

Executive Yuan: The highest administrative organ of the nation.

Legislative Yuan: The highest legislative organ of the nation; sessions are held twice a year.

Judicial Yuan: The highest judicial organ of the nation.

Examination Yuan: Supervises examinations for entry into public offices.

Control Yuan: This group is elected by local councils to investigate the work of the Executive Yuan and the ministries and executives. Meetings are held once a month.

Political Party

The major ruling party in Taiwan is Kuomingtang (KTM), and the main opposition party is the Democratic Progressive party (DPP). There are approximately 20 political parties in Taiwan after the liberalization of the restriction.

Trade Flows

The top five export partners for Taiwan are: U.S.A., Japan, Hong Kong, West Germany, and U.K. The top five import partners are: Japan, U.S.A., West Germany, Hong Kong, and Australia.

Top Import/Export Commodities

The top export commodities include the following: electronic products, garments, yarn and fabric, footwear, metal products, toys and sporting goods, machinery, plastic products, transportation, plywood, furniture, and electrical machinery and apparatus.

The top import commodities include the following: machinery, electrical machinery and apparatus, transportation equipment, crude oil, electronic products, chemicals, iron and steel, food, beverages and tobacco products, pulp, paper and allied products, scientific measuring and controlling instruments.

Finance and Investment Policies

The Statute for Encouragement of Investment and the Statutes for Investment by Foreign Nationals and by Overseas Chinese are the major laws governing foreign investment in Taiwan. Reinvestment of earnings is encouraged, although repatriation of earnings and capital from approved investments is permitted. Earnings can be repatriated within six months after being declared to authorities. Limitations on the transfer of investment capital out of Taiwan of annual installments of 15% were eliminated in November 1986. The only restriction remaining is that capital gains derived from an increase in land value cannot be taken out of Taiwan; however, the authorities are also planning to remove this restriction.

Firms with 45% or more of foreign investment are free from nationalization for 20 years, although no foreign-investment firm, even with foreign ownership below 45%, has ever been nationalized or expropriated. U.S. investors have never filed an Overseas Private Investment Corporation insurance claim for an investment in Taiwan.

Policies to Attract New Business

Preferred Foreign Investment Projects

The most favorable industries for overseas capital investment in ROC include machinery manufacturing, the electronics and information industry, chemicals, and technical services. A brief description of each follows:

- Machinery manufacturing – complete plant, high precision machine tools, automotive parts and components, steel mold, casting, precision forging, solar energy equipment, industrial robots, and automatic manufacturing system.

- Electronics and information industry – sophisticated products for industrial use.

- Chemicals – specialty chemicals for industrial use.

- Technical services – technical know-how or patent rights licensing and technical assistance in plant construction, design, and engineering work.

Investment Incentives and Privileges

Overseas investments are accorded the same incentives and privileges as accorded to domestic investments by Chinese nationals. Additional incentives and privileges include the following:

- Overseas investors may have 100% ownership of the enterprises they invest in.

- All net profits and interest earnings can be remitted.

- Repatriation of 100% of the total investment capital is allowed at the expiration of one year after the commencement of operation.

- Protection against government expropriation or requisition is for 20 years if the overseas investment in an enterprise is, and continues to be, 45% or more of the total registered capital.

Tax Incentives

A number of tax incentives are offered. Some of these include the following:

- In the case of a newly established productive enterprise eligible for encouragement, the investor may choose to enjoy a five-year holiday on profit-seeking enterprise income tax or accelerated depreciation of fixed assets. When increasing capital to expand machinery and equipment, the enterprise may choose to benefit from either a profit-seeking enterprise income tax exemption for four years or accelerated depreciation of fixed assets on the expanded portion.

- Enterprise income tax and surtaxes on big trading companies, venture capital investment enterprises, special capital- or technology-intensive enterprises, and important technology-based enterprises designated by the government are limited to 20% of their taxable income. A 25% maximum level for general productive enterprises.

- A profit-seeking enterprise organized as a company limited by shares, publicly listed on the stock market in the form of registered certificates, is entitled to a 15% reduction on the profit-seeking enterprise income.

- A 20% withholding tax is levied on dividends for nonresident overseas investors who derive the dividends from a company established in accordance with the Statute for Investment by Foreign Nationals and by Overseas Chinese.

Free Trade Zones/Special Economic Zones

Export processing zones are designed for export industries. Three export processing zones have been developed at Kaohsiung, Nantze, and Taichung. Customs duty on machinery, equipment, and raw materials imported by factories in the zones are exempt.

Investors may purchase standard factory buildings in the zones and borrow money from local banks at favorable interest rates.

The EPZ Administration is authorized to handle all phases of operations within the zone including investment application processing and approval, import and export licensing, foreign exchange settlement, company registration, construction licensing, and customs clearances. The EPZ Administration has raised the minimum capital requirement for establishing a plant in the EPZs from NT $6 million to NT $20 million.

APPROACHING THE MARKET

Foreign Trade and Investment Decision-Making Infrastructure

Trading with Taiwan is becoming easier and more convenient for foreign business people and manufacturers. The ROC or Taiwan categorizes imports into controlled and permissible items. With the liberalization of the economy, the government has been allowing the import of a larger range of products each year. Currently, only 257 items are listed as controlled. All of the remaining Import Tariff and Classification of Import and Export Commodities listings are permissible.

Taiwan's government initiated 12 new development projects in 1973 to upgrade the nation's development and provide better lives for its people. Before its completion, the government decided to initiate 14 additional construction projects. These latter projects are intended to improve the island's infrastructure and sustain future economic growth and development. They represent a total government investment of over US $25 billion.

In January 1991, Taiwan's government approved a plan to pump NT $303 billion into the country's roads, phones, transit services, and environmental facilities over the next six years. With 779 projects ranging from an extensive subway system to nuclear reactors, the government is leading Taiwan into its most ambitious renewal program ever. The government has a "Don't Buy Japanese" policy, which gives the biggest plus to the U.S. investors.

State and Private Services

Market Research

The China External Trade Development Council (CETRA), a nonprofit, independent trade promotion organization supported by public officials and local business associations, offers market information to companies doing business in Taiwan. In addition, Gaynor Eastern International, International Research Associates (Asia) Ltd., Rockwell International Taiwan Co., Ltd., and other U.S. and local corporations offer a wide range of services from product and consumer research to trade survey, advertising research, media research, and credit information. The American Institute in Taiwan supplies the U.S. Department of Commerce with information on the Taiwan economy as well as commercial and market studies. A limited range of market research is also available to U.S. companies through the U.S. Department of Commerce.

Incorporation/Registration

An overseas investor should submit his or her investment application to the Investment Commission (IC) of the Ministry of Economic Affairs (MOEA). After the approval is granted, the following procedures must be fulfilled:

1. Remit capital into Taiwan and notify the IC of the remittance.

2. Apply to the IC for company registration.

3. Apply to the local authorities for registration as a profit-seeking enterprise.

4. Purchase or lease a plant site.

5. Apply to the local authorities for the license for the construction of factory buildings and for registration of the establishment of the factory.

6. Apply to Taipower's regional office for supply of electricity.

Foreign investments not meeting the criteria for FIA (Foreign Investment Agency) companies do not enjoy repatriation rights or other investment incentives. These non-FIA invested firms must apply to MOEA's Department of Commerce for registration as a business enterprise in Taiwan.

Setting Up Business Operations

Forms of Business Organization

Limited liability company. The limited company is organized by not less than five and no more than 21 shareholders; each shareholder is liable to the amount of contributed capital. The company limited by shares is similar to a U.S. corporation and is the most common type of business enterprise in Taiwan. More importantly, it is the only business form that is eligible for tax and other incentives under the Statute for Encouragement of Investment.

Branches of foreign corporations. A foreign corporation may establish a branch in Taiwan by obtaining the authorities's recognition of the existence of the company as a foreign entity and by registering with MOEA. A foreign firm wishing to set up a branch must provide MOEA with detailed information on their parent firm, including: date of incorporation; authorized capital; classes of stock; location of the headquarters and of the proposed Taiwan branch; and names, nationalities, and residence of the directors, other key officers in the parent firm, and the designated representatives in Taiwan.

Branches are not eligible for tax incentives or other benefits under the Statute for Encouragement of Investment.

Sole traders and partnerships. Taiwan law does not recognize businesses operated as a sole proprietorship or partnership as legal persons. Hence, investors in these types of organizations have unlimited liability in the enterprise's debts and obligations. Although no law prohibits foreign investors from registering under these forms, such businesses are unattractive due to their ineligibility for investment incentives under the Statute for Encouragement of Investment.

Representative offices. These offices are permitted to engage in such areas as the procurement and inspection of goods, the signing of contracts, bidding, and handling litigious and nonlitigious matters. They may not, however, conduct profit-seeking commercial activities or act as a principal in any domestic business transaction in Taiwan. Each office must also be headed by a representative who is a Chinese national or a foreigner who holds an Alien Resident Certificate.

Sales Promotion, Fairs, Conferences, and Advertising

The China External Trade Development Council (CETRA) is the premier trade-promotion agency in the ROC. It offers a wide range of information and service. Far East Trade Service, a sister organization of CETRA, is a nonprofit entity assisting CETRA in the promotion of Taiwan products at home and abroad. Another sister organization of CETRA is Taipei World Trade Center (TWTC). Its exhibition hall has been managed by CETRA since its completion in 1986.

Many Taiwan advertising agencies function specifically to assist in the preparation and placement of advertisements in the mass communications media. The annual *Taiwan Buyers' Guide* provides a list of nearly 24 such organizations. A number of U.S. advertising agencies are located in Taiwan.

Agents and Distributors

There are two basic kinds of purchasing agents in Taiwan. The first is a commission agent who acts on behalf of the buyer. This agent will typically locate a supplier, assist in business negotiations, and coordinate inspection of goods before shipment. The functions of the second kind of agent are similar to those of a trading company. The agent first receives a letter of credit directly from a foreign buyer and then purchases the specified goods for subsequent sale to that buyer. This agent, who has title to the goods and responsibility for product quality, generally acts as the shipper or exporter.

Consignment and Re-Export

Under Taiwan's present duty rebate system, import duties levied on raw materials destined for local processing and re-export are comparable with duties levied on general imports. When these materials have been reprocessed and shipped, the duties paid out may be refunded or credited to the re-exporter usually after a four- to six-month delay. The authorities have begun to implement a proposal to abolish the duty rebate system with the goal of improving efficiency, reducing costs, and modernizing the customs service. Under the proposed system, the percentage of import tax refunded to exporters will be gradually reduced and offset by continued reductions in tariff rates.

Setting Up Offices, Retail Stores, and Service Facilities

Real estate. Foreign manufacturers are permitted to own land and factories in Taiwan. Land experts at IDIC can assist investors in locating plant sites and in negotiating the purchase of private land.

Zoning. Over the years, the government of the ROC has been one of the foremost pioneers in the development of free trade zones. These facilities, which include export processing zones and science-based industrial parks, continue to be of great benefit to overseas investors and buyers. The export processing zones were designed to cater to the needs of foreign and domestic investors.

Land in the special zones is not for sale, but is leased to investors by the authority. Standard factory buildings are available to purchase in EPZs and three industrial estates.

Transportation and Freight (Air/Sea)

Taiwan is one of Asia's leading transshipment centers, with a well-developed infrastructure for sea and air transport capable of handling an enormous volume of international cargo traffic. As a result, almost all of the major international air and ocean freight carriers and forwarders are represented here.

Air freight. Some 186,803 metric tons of freight arrived in Taiwan by air in 1988, while 298,241 metric tons left the island during the same period. This cargo went through Chiang Kai-shek International Airport. Leading carriers and forwarders generally have offices in almost all major cities on the island.

Ocean freight. ROC is now the fourth largest cargo handler in the world, ranking behind only the United States, Japan, and the UK. Kaohsiung is the third busiest port in terms of overall container volume.

INVESTMENT CLIMATE

Privatization, Investment Protection, and Dispute Settlement

A continuing liberalization campaign will accelerate the door-opening policy on foreign bank operations and relax restrictions. In addition, it will bring more U.S. insurance companies to Taiwan and allow foreign securities firms to participate in local market transactions. Investment authorities are trying to further improve the local investment climate by adopting a "negative list" specifically identifying a limited number of industries closed to foreign investment.

Investment disputes are not common. In August 1982, a U.S. manufacturer pulled out of a joint venture with several state enterprises to manufacture heavy trucks, the result of a disagreement with the authorities over the extent of import protection to be provided; the U.S. company was compensated. In another case currently pending in the courts, a U.S. tissue paper manufacturer is in a dispute with its local partner over the level of royalty payments.

Taiwan has concluded few bilateral investment agreements. Under the terms of the 1948 Friendship, Commerce, and Navigation Treaty with the United States, enforced in substance through the Taiwan Relations Act, U.S. investors are generally accorded national treatment and are provided a number of protections, including protection against expropriation.

Joint Ventures and Wholly Owned Subsidiaries

Foreign investors planning to cooperate with Taiwan companies can establish joint ventures with one or more domestic partners. In most instances, it is advisable for foreign firms to seek FIA status for such joint venture arrangements.

Subsidiaries often give foreign companies a greater degree of control and help avoid some of the restrictions inherent in partnerships. Moreover, they are more effective in protecting what is often very substantial capital investment. With wholly owned Taiwan-based subsidiaries, it is essential to obtain FIA status.

Cooperation Agreements, Leasing, and Franchising

Although domestic franchising in Taiwan is booming, the authorities strictly control foreign franchises through stringent foreign exchange controls and foreign investment regulations. In accordance with general foreign investment policy, the authorities are most likely to approve franchise proposals that introduce new technology to Taiwan or improve the island's standard of living. Taiwan has no legislation directed specifically at franchising. In order to implement any franchise agreement, the foreign franchiser must register trademarks with Taiwan's National Bureau of Standards. Also, under the Statute for Technical Cooperation, the franchiser must apply to the IC for approval of royalty or franchise fee payments in foreign exchange.

Taxation and Regulatory Conditions

Sources of Income Liable to Taxation

Nineteen taxes are levied in Taiwan, each under the jurisdiction of a separate tax law. Of these 19 taxes, eight are direct taxes (income, rural land, land-value, land-value increment, inheritance, mine lot, house, and deed taxes) and 11 are indirect taxes (customs duty, commodity, business, salt, stamp, vehicle license, security transaction, banquet, entertainment, slaughter, and harbor taxes).

Company Tax

A business tax is levied on the monthly gross business revenues of all profit-seeking enterprises in Taiwan. The business tax is assessed against a transaction's gross value and has varying rates of 0.75% to 45%, depending on the type of business the taxable enterprise is engaged in.

Personal Income Tax

Personal income tax is levied on an individual's gross consolidated income (with a few limited exceptions) derived from sources within Taiwan or paid for services rendered within Taiwan. Rates range from 6% to 60%. Tax is withheld on all Taiwan income, including dividends, at a rate of 20% to 35% for the nonresident taxpayer and 10% to 15% for the resident taxpayer.

Property Tax

A commodity tax is currently levied on 19 product categories sold for consumption in Taiwan including cigarettes, foreign wines and beer, electric appliances, cars, and cosmetics. Rates range from 2% to 120% and are applied to both domestic manufactures and imports.

FINANCING AND CAPITAL MARKETS

Banking and Other Financial Institutions

Taiwan has a Central Bank and more than 680 other domestic banking institutions, including both commercial and specialized banks. There are also 74 registered credit cooperatives, 282 agricultural credit unions, and 22 fishery credit unions.

The Central Bank. The Central Bank essentially performs all of the functions normally associated with central banks in other countries. It has made several changes in the nation's foreign exchange system, such as the July 1987 rule abolishing the requirement of individuals and companies to convert their foreign exchange holdings into NT dollars.

Specialized banks. The Bank of Communications, the Export-Import Bank, and the Farmer's Bank of China are all examples of such institutions.

Foreign banks. These banks are playing an increasingly important role in the financial sector.

Offshore banking. The ROC government created the legal framework for offshore banking in mid-1984.

Payment Modalities

Taiwan and the United States maintain an agreement pertaining to investment guarantees, that serves as the basis for the U.S. Overseas Private Investment Corporation (OPIC) program in Taiwan. Taiwan plans to establish a similar investment guarantee program as part of its effort to promote Taiwan investment in the Caribbean and Southeast Asian region, where authorities are currently negotiating several bilateral investment agreements. Taiwan signed an investment agreement with Paraguay in 1975 and with Singapore in April 1990.

OPIC insurance programs are available to U.S. investors in Taiwan. In 1989, OPIC insurance coverage for U.S. investment in Taiwan totaled US $168 million for inconvertibility, US $174 million for expropriation, and US $73 million for war.

Financial Market Operations

Money Market

A money market was established in 1976. The Ministry of Finance designated the Bank of Taiwan, the International Commercial Bank of China, and the Bank of Communications to organize three corporations to act as money-market dealers and brokers. The first of these, Chung Hsing Bills Finance Corporation, was formed in 1976. The other two, International Bills Finance Corporation and Chung Hwa Bills Finance Corporation, entered the market later. These corporations are currently authorized to underwrite commercial paper for private-sector businesses and act as brokers and intermediaries for government securities and interbank loans. In addition, they can buy and sell government securities, banker's acceptances, and negotiable certificates of deposit issued by banks.

Securities Market

The Taiwan Stock Exchange was established in 1961. This exchange, along with brokers, dealers, underwriters, and other related entities, is subject to regulation by the Securities and Exchange Commission of the Ministry of Finance. A recent announcement by the Securities and Exchange Commission allowing foreign brokerage firms meeting certain paid-in capital requirements to set up Taiwan branches should benefit both the industry and Taiwan investors. The ROC government plans to allow direct investment by foreign institutional investors in ROC portfolio securities, as well as to permit direct investment by individual foreign investors.

Gold Market

The government has liberalized restrictions related to the domestic gold market. A long standing import ban on gold intended for sale to the general public has been lifted, and domestic transactions in the metal have been legalized.

Futures Market

The legal status of futures operations remains ambiguous at present. Futures trading actually began in Taiwan in 1971, when a U.S. futures company set up a branch office in Taipei. Subsequently, three other companies were established, but all four essentially confined their activities to dealing in agricultural futures and hedging. Although no legislation was passed to regularize their status, the liberalization of foreign exchange control in July of 1987 encouraged a number of Hong Kong futures firms to enter into cooperative arrangements with counterparts in Taiwan. To provide for more effective regulation and control in a sector critically important to the island's trade and economy, the Ministry of Economic Affairs has drafted a Foreign Futures Trading Law. Once this law is approved by the Executive Yuan and enacted into law by the Legislative Yuan, futures market trading should begin to play a more productive role in the nation's development.

LICENSING, PATENTS, AND TRADEMARKS

Licensing Policy, Procedures, and Payments

Foreign corporations can furnish technical knowledge, patents, or trademarks to an existing Taiwan firm as capital investment or for a fixed royalty. The Statute for Technical Cooperation governs licensing agreements involving foreign exchange payments and is administered by the MOEA's Investment Commission (IC). In order to repatriate royalties and technical assistance fees in foreign exchange, the foreign licensor must first submit a technical cooperation application and the proposed licensing agreement to the IC. These documents should detail the products, services, technical skills, or patent rights involved, royalties, method of payment, and duration of the agreement. Although the authorities do not set royalty amounts, the IC must approve the rate negotiated between the licensor and licensee.

Trademark, Patent, and Copyright Protection

Foreign firms wishing to register their trademarks in Taiwan must delegate an agent with a domicile or place of business in Taiwan. Taiwan's National Bureau of Standards grants trademark protection for specially distinctive words, devices, marks, or combinations thereof. Trademark applications are normally processed in three to four months. The granting of a trademark confers upon the registered owner the exclusive right of its use for 10 years.

Foreign patent holders may file for a Taiwan patent on any new invention possessing industrial value through a registered Taiwan patent attorney. The term of a Taiwan patent calculated from the date of publication is 15 years for inventions, 10 years for new utility models, and five years for new designs.

VISITING AND LOCATING

General Travel Checklist

Visas

Two basic types of nonofficial visas are available to foreign visitors, depending upon the nature and duration of their intended visits. They are resident and visitor visas. Visitor visas are granted to foreign nationals who wish to visit Taiwan and are valid for three months from the date of issue and are good for single stays in Taiwan for periods of up to sixty days. Multiple-entry visitor visas can be granted to the representatives of foreign companies that have purchased a total of more than US $1 million worth of Taiwan products in the preceding 12 months or that have bought an annual average of US $1 million worth over the preceding three years. Resident visas are issued to foreign nationals wishing to stay in the ROC for more than six months.

Currency

The New Taiwan dollar is the official currency of the ROC. It is circulated in one-, five-, and ten-dollar coins, and fifty, one-hundred, five-hundred, and one-thousand dollar notes. Up to NT $8,000 or US $5,000 can be brought into the ROC by a foreign visitor.

Getting Around

Taiwan has two international airports, Chiang Kai-shek International and Kaohsiung International. The CKS International Airport is 40 kilometers from Taipei. Under normal conditions, it takes around 45 minutes to reach the city center. A limousine airport bus is available to take visitors either to or from the airport at a cost of NT $72. The taxi fare, in most instances, should be around NT $800 and is negotiable.

Bus services in the island's major cities are quite extensive but can be incomprehensible to the foreign visitor. A long-distance bus system run by the Taiwan Auto-Transport Company enables people to travel anywhere on the island. The Taiwan Railway Administration operates an extensive rail network. Reservations can be booked at major railway stations three days before departure.

Accommodations and Housing

Taiwan has a large number of international- and domestic-standard hotels, hostels, and inns. In general, five-star hotel accommodations cost around NT $4,500 per night, while tourist-standard hotel rates run between NT $1,000 and NT $2,500. For those who plan to stay in Taiwan on a long-term basis, a wide selection of apartments and houses is available. Rental costs vary considerably, depending on location and size.

Electricity Supply

Electricity is supplied at 110 volts, 60 hertz. Most sockets are of the two-pin, flat variety. Industries have access to 220 volts, 60 hertz and 440 volts, 60 hertz service.

Telecom, Postal, and Courier Services

In general, Taiwan's telecommunications and postal systems are efficient and convenient. Some of the services available are explained below.

Telephone service. The charge for the installation of private and office phones is NT $10,000. Basic minimum monthly charge is NT $333 for business use. Public phone rates are NT $1 for three minutes. Domestic long distance calls may be direct dialed on private phones or made on the public pay phones. Direct dialing on international calls is also available for a number of countries.

Cable and telegraph services. The ITA offers complete international cable and domestic telegraphic services.

Facsimile and telex services. Direct transmission is available to many countries in the world. Most companies and major hotels have telex facilities.

Postal service. All post offices on the island are open six days a week from 8:30 a.m. to 5:30 p.m. The basic rate for ordinary domestic surface mail is only NT $3, although an additional NT $4.5 is added to the basic charge for express mail.

Courier service. Most of the leading international courier services have set up operations in Taiwan in the last few years.

Business Cards

Formal business introductions in Taiwan are not complete without an exchange of business cards. It is advisable for foreign visitors to have their cards printed in both English and Chinese.

Business Hours

Banks are open from 9:00 a.m. to 3:30 p.m. on Monday through Friday and 9:00 a.m. to noon on Saturday. Most offices and factories are open from 9:00 a.m. to noon and then reopen from 1:30 p.m. to 5:30 p.m. on Monday through Friday. Saturday hours are from 9:00 a.m. to 12:30 p.m. Government offices are open from 8:30 a.m. to noon and then reopen from 1:30 p.m. to 5:30 p.m. on Monday through Friday. Saturday hours are from 8:30 a.m. to 12:00 p.m.

Tipping

In most instances, tipping is not necessary. A 10% service charge is usually added to restaurant and hotel bills, eliminating the need for gratuities. Porters at hotel and airports customarily receive tips for their services. Approximately NT $50 to NT $100 per item of luggage is acceptable.

What to Wear

The weather in Taiwan is relatively humid, accompanied by frequent rain. The uncomfortable heat during the May to October period makes light clothing essential, while a light jacket and sweater are necessary in winter months.

Health Care

As in many other tropical and subtropical areas, tap water in Taiwan should be boiled before drinking. Visitors should also take special care to wash all fruits and vegetables before eating and avoid eating in any of the island's countless street stalls. There are numerous international standard private and public hospitals and clinics. The majority of doctors and dentists in Taiwan speak good English. Traditional-style Chinese medicine, including both herbal medicine and acupuncture, is widely practiced. Many Western brand-name pharmaceuticals are sold in Taiwan. Emergency medical treatment can be obtained by dialing 119.

The Media

There are 93 daily newspapers in Taiwan with a total circulation of around 3.8 million. The English-language *China News* and *China Post* are both published daily. Presently, the island has three television stations and 188 radio stations, including ICRT, an English-language station.

Availability of Foreign Products

A vast array of foreign products can be purchased in Taiwan, including foodstuffs, cigarettes, beverages, liquors, cosmetics, and clothing. Many items are available primarily at supermarkets and departments stores in the large cities.

Shopping

Taiwan is home to numerous large department stores and supermarkets, as well as countless small retail shops and fascinating Chinese markets. Although prices for certain items tend to be high, the cost of most Taiwan-made goods is relatively modest. Taiwan electronic goods and clothing are usually good bargains for the shopper from abroad. However, the best bargains on the island are found in the street-side markets that come to life in the evenings. The prices are generally low, and vendors sell virtually everything imaginable.

Dining Out

Chinese cuisine ranks among the best in the world, and there is no better place to sample its infinite variety than in Taiwan. In the island's countless large and small restaurants, specialties from almost every region can be found. Western food is gaining in popularity; many Western-restaurants and foreign fast food chains have set up branches in Taiwan's large cities recently.

Entertainment

Major cities in Taiwan have excellent entertainment facilities, including cozy Western-style pubs. In Taipei, there are also many bars catering to Western tastes.

For Westerners looking to experience the exotic East, there are countless Japanese-style karaoke where guests are encouraged to sing to their favorite songs on stage. The island's Chinese-style nightclubs are expensive but offer visitors a fascinating insight into contemporary Taiwan life and culture.

Sightseeing and Tourist Information

The Taiwan Tourism Bureau maintains an information service for the convenience of those visiting Taiwan. The Tourist Information Hotline is open every day of the year from 8:00 a.m. to 8:00 p.m. It is staffed by knowledgeable individuals fluent in English and a number of other languages. The Tourist Information Hotline number is (02)717-3737.

There are many tourist spots of great cultural interest and natural beauty scattered around the island. In order to avoid the crowds, it is best to try to visit these sites during the week, rather than on Saturday or Sunday.

Recreational Opportunities

Foreign visitors will find that Taiwan offers ample opportunities for recreation and exercise. At least 12 major hotels in Taipei maintain exercise facilities for their guests. For those who plan to reside on the island for relatively long periods of time, the Taiwan Youth Program Association offers comprehensive sports and recreation programs catering to the foreign community. Among the many places in Taipei where outdoor exercise is performed are the New Park, the grounds of the Chung Cheng Memorial Hall, the compound of the Sun Yat-sen Memorial Hall, and the hilly Grand Hotel area.

The Short-Term Business Visitor

Airlines

Taipei's CKS International Airport is served by 17 airlines — China Airlines, Cathay Pacific Airways, Cargolux Airlines, Flying Tigers Line, Garuda Indonesian Airways, Japan Asia Airways, Korean Air, KLM Royal Dutch Airlines, Malaysian Airlines System, Martinair Holland, Northwest Orient Airlines, United Airlines, Philippine Airlines, Royal Brunei Airlines, Singapore Airlines, South African Airways, and Thai Airways. Kaohsiung International Airport is also served by two airlines—China Airlines and Japan Asia Airways.

Employment and Labor Relations

Taiwan's current supply of unskilled workers is inadequate. Acute shortages of unskilled labor will persist in labor-intensive industries such as textiles, footwear, and electronics assembly as the average skill level of Taiwan workers increases in response to the economic shift toward capital- and technology-intensive areas. Despite the shortages, labor remains Taiwan's leading resource because workers are diligent and adept at learning new skills. Almost all prospective workers have a minimum of ninth grade education with an emphasis on technical and vocational training. Average wage rates are rising with the increase of Taiwan's standard of living and the skill level of its workers. The island's previous labor cost advantages are steadily diminishing vis-a-vis its less developed Asian neighbors.

Taiwan's labor force is becoming increasingly assertive although labor-management relations are still generally very good. The growing political significance attached to workers' needs and demands is evidenced by the establishment of a cabinet-level council of labor affairs in August 1987. Strikes and lockouts are permitted by law in nongovernmental enterprises other than utilities, transportation, and communications, except in times of national emergency or during conciliation and arbitration proceedings. Unionism is not prevalent in Taiwan.

Conditions of Work

Regular working hours are eight hours a day and no more than 48 hours a week. Overtime cannot exceed three hours a day and 46 hours a month for a male and two hours a day and 24 hours a month for a female. A worker must be given a day off every seven consecutive days. Employees are also entitled to leave for all national holidays, including Labor Day, and must be granted annual leave after one year of service. An employee in the ROC may voluntarily retire at age 55 after 15 years of service or at any time after 25 years of service.

Employment and Medical Insurance

Almost all employees in the Republic of China are included in a labor insurance program covering maternity, injury, sickness, disability, old age, death, and occupational hazards. Under the provisions of this labor-insurance program, any establishment employing five or more workers must enter into labor insurance contracts with the Labor Insurance Bureau for each employee over age 14 and below age 60. In terms of coverage and premium payment, labor insurance is currently divided into ordinary-risk and occupational-risk insurance.

Training

Taiwan's educational system emphasizes both the needs of individual and the requirements of the society and economy. Taiwan has succeeded in creating one of the best trained labor forces to be found anywhere. In almost any field, foreign investors will be able to find personnel with the proper training. Moreover, in addition to this basic competency, members of the Taiwan work force have the kind of educational preparation and cultural background that makes it easy for them adapt to new situations and "grow with the job."

TAIWAN

KEY CONTACTS

American Embassy Contacts

American Institute in Taiwan
Taipei Office
7 Lane 134
Hsin Yi Road, Section 3
   Tel: 886/2-709-2000
   Telex: 23890 USTRADE

American Institute in Taiwan
Washington Office
1700 N. Moore Street Suite 1700
Arlington, VA 22209-1996
   Tel: 703/525-8474
   Fax: 703/841-1385

American Institute in Taiwan
Commercial Unit - Room 3207
International Trade Building
Taipei World Trade Center
333 Keelung Road, Section 1
Taipei 10548
   Tel: 886/2-720-1550
   Fax: 886/2-757-7162

American Institute in Taiwan
Kaohsiung Office
3d Floor, Number 2
Chung Cheng
3d Road
   Tel: 07/251-2444/7

Taiwan Desk - Room 2327
U.S. Department of Commerce
14th and Constitution Avenue, NW
Washington, DC 20230
Tel: 202/377-4957
Fax: 202/377-4453

Office of Major Projects - Room 2015 B
U.S. Department of Commerce
14th and Constitution Avenue, NW
Washington, DC 20230
Tel: 202/377-2000

Coordination Council for North American Affairs (CCNAA)
Economic Division - Room 420
4301 Connecticut Avenue, NW
Washington, DC 20008
Tel: 202/686-6400
Fax: 202/363-6294

China External Trade and Development Council (CETRA)
New York Merchandise Mart
14th Floor
41 Madison Avenue
New York, NY 10010
Tel: 212/532-7055

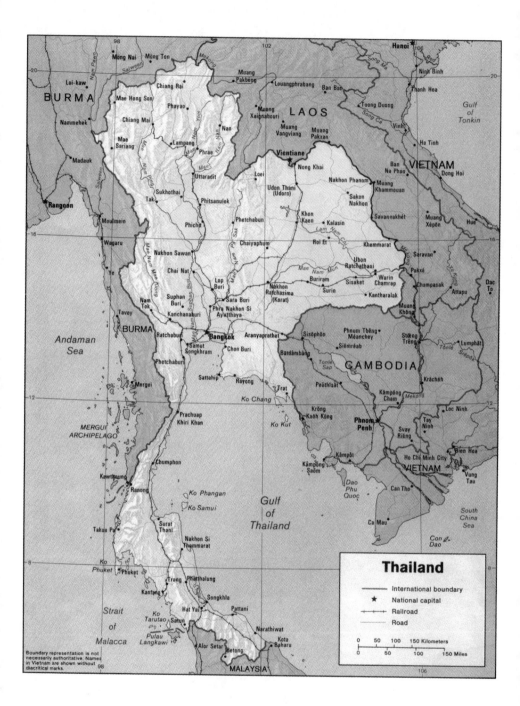

THAILAND

THAILAND
In a Nutshell

Population (1992)	58,800,000	**Urban Population** 21.2%
Main Urban Areas Bangkok	5,174,682	**Percentage of Total** 8.8

Land Area
198,455 square miles
514,000 square kilometers

Comparable European State
Slightly larger than Spain

Comparable U.S. State
Slightly more than twice the size of Wyoming

Language
Thai, English

Common Business Language
English

Currency
Baht (B)

Best Air Connection
Seattle-Taipei-Bangkok (daily)
Seattle-Tokyo-Bangkok (daily)
Los Angeles-Seoul-Bangkok (Mon., Thurs., and Sat.)
Thai Airlines 800/426-5204

Best Hotel
Hyatt Regency
($224/night as of 2/92)

InterContinental
($198/night as of 2/92)

CHAPTER CONTENTS

INTRODUCTION AND REGIONAL ORIENTATION

Geographical and Historical Background

Thailand, formerly known as Siam, lies in the heart of mainland Southeast Asia. It is the only country in South Asia and Southeast Asia that was never colonized by a European power.

Demographics

Thailand has a population of 57 million, 90% of whom are Buddhists. The country has a large, well-assimilated Chinese element, constituting one of the main engines of industrial growth.

Socioeconomic Indicators and Conditions

The population is predominantly rural and most heavily concentrated in the rice-growing areas of the center, northeast, and north. With one of the world's fastest growing populations, the government sponsored a successful family planning program reducing the annual population growth rate from 3.1% in 1960 to less than 1.6% in 1987. Life expectancy increased from 51 years in 1960 to 64.2 years in 1979.

Universal free education is a high state priority. Education is the third largest item in the Thai budget, accounting for over 15% of the total. In 1985, 96% of primary and 30% of secondary school-age children were enrolled in school and 5.7% were in universities or colleges. The adult literacy rate is 90%.

While some 80% of the population continues to live in rural areas, the relative importance of the agricultural sector as a contributor to GDP has declined. Agriculture accounted for 15% of GDP in the 1980s, down from 23% a decade earlier.

As industrialization takes hold, the educated people in Thailand rely less on government and the armed services as routes to wealth and power. The new generation looks increasingly to business, banking, and financial services.

Thailand's policy of promoting export-led growth through processing and manufacturing has led to significantly higher income levels in Bangkok and a few other areas where manufacturing and tourism are major activities. Elsewhere, it has been much slower. Information on income distribution is not available. Nonetheless, it is estimated that the per capita income in the Bangkok area is probably around US $3,000, several times the per capita income in some poor up-country areas. Despite widespread poverty in the countryside, Thailand's relatively high productivity in food production assures that malnutrition is far less common than in most developing countries.

Thailand's labor force grew 3.9% during 1990, reaching approximately 31 million. Official unemployment rose to 4.9% by the end of 1990. The extent of underemployment is difficult to measure, but it appears to be extensive, particularly in rural areas.

Trends in Consumer Demand

The industrialization of Thailand and its concurrent economic development brought changes in Thai eating habits. This is seen in the popularity of western-style (including fast food) restaurants and in displacement of traditional "wet markets" by modern supermarkets.

Political/Institutional Infrastructure

Political Organization

Under the 1978 constitution, Thailand is a constitutional monarchy. The king is the formal head of state, although he has little power. However, he is an important symbol of national identity and unity. A 14-member Privy Council is appointed by the king to advise him and, under certain conditions, to appoint a regent for the exercise of royal powers.

The constitution designates the National Assembly as the legislative body, composed of a popularly elected lower house and an upper house appointed by the prime minister. The office of prime minister is the center of political power. The prime minister heads the cabinet and may personally select a cabinet of up to 44 ministers and deputy ministers.

The armed forces have traditionally exercised a pervasive role in Thai politics. Since the establishment of a constitutional monarchy in 1932, Thailand has undergone more than a dozen military coups or coup attempts. The most recent was in February 1991, which overthrew Prime Minister Chatichai Choonhavan. Mr. Chatichai took office in August 1988 as the first prime minister since 1976 to be an elected member of Parliament.

Federal/Regional/Municipal Organization

Thailand's 73 provinces include the metropolis of greater Bangkok. Provincial governors are appointed by the Ministry of Interior, which also appoints district officers throughout the country for the districts into which provinces are subdivided for second-level administration. Larger towns are administered through the shared authority of elected municipal assemblies and district officers.

Trade Flows

Top 10 Export Commodities

In 1989, the top 10 export commodities included the following: garments, rice, gems and jewelry, rubber, tapioca products, computers and parts, canned seafood, raw sugar and molasses, integrated circuits, and fabrics and yarns.

THAILAND
Import Trade Partners
(1989 US$ Billion)

Japan	$8.3
United States	$2.7
Singapore	$1.9
West Germany	$1.4
Taiwan	$1.3
China	$0.8
South Korea	$0.7
United Kingdom	$0.6
Malaysia	$0.6
Australia	$0.5

THAILAND
Export Trade Partners
(1989 US$ Billion)

United States	$4.3
Japan	$3.6
Singapore	$1.5
Netherlands	$1.0
West Germany	$0.8
United Kingdom	$0.8
Hong Kong	$0.8
China	$0.7
Malaysia	$0.6
France	$0.4

Finance and Investment Policies

The Investment Promotion Act of 1977 provides the basic framework for investment. The Alien Business Law of 1966, the Alien Occupation Law of 1973, and the Immigration Law of 1979 impose certain restrictions on investors.

Under the Alien Business Law of 1972, non-Thais are prohibited from majority ownership of companies engaged in a broad range of agricultural, industrial, commercial, and service industries (including law, architecture, accounting, and advertising). Some foreign-owned companies, which predated the 1972 law, were allowed to continue after registering with the government.

Despite this prohibition, companies which are majority-owned by aliens may still be established if they gain approval of the Board of Investment. Exporting, mining, textile manufacturing, and companies engaged in service industries not specifically excluded may also be granted government approval, even if they are majority-owned by aliens.

The Board of Investment offers incentives to Thai and foreign investors who commit to, for example, exporting at least 80% of their production or locating outside the Bangkok area. There are also attractive opportunities for investing at the Securities Exchange of Thailand.

An investor willing to accept a minority position in line with government ownership limits, which vary according to industry sector, may establish or engage in business in Thailand. An alien business can lose its alien character and thereby fall outside the application of the Alien Business Law through transfer of a majority of shares, partnership interests, or management to Thai persons.

Policies to Attract New Business

Preferred Foreign Investment Projects

Principal projects for foreign investment include the oil and gas industry and manufacturing, particularly in food processing, textiles and garments, and electronics.

Investment Incentives and Privileges

Thailand provides promotional assistance to long-term foreign private investment, particularly to projects which are labor-intensive, export-oriented, and agro-based. Moreover, Thailand has a long history of accommodating foreign business interests.

Foreign investors in Thailand generally have the same basic rights as Thai nationals unless those rights are specifically reserved for nationals. In most sectors with restrictions on foreign majority positions, foreigners are permitted a minority position. Foreigners are not permitted to own land except in cases where foreign-owned projects enjoy investment privileges including land ownership.

Under the terms of the 1966 U.S.-Thai Treaty of Amity and Economic Relations, Americans generally are free to own up to 100% of their businesses. However, if investment promotion privileges are desired — tax holidays, duty-free importation of equipment, free entry of necessary expatriate staff, right to buy land, and the like — negotiations must be undertaken with the Board of Investment regarding the extent of U.S. equity shareholding.

A wholly export-oriented foreign investment may still be 100% foreign-owned, but the percentages decrease to 49%, depending on the percentage of output of the investment destined to be sold in the domestic market and other factors. Foreign investment in areas of high national priority attracts extra incentives, usually by means of extensions of the tax holiday period. The prospective investor should seek advice from the United States and Foreign and Commercial Service (USFCS) Bangkok and the Board of Investment.

Tax Incentives

Thailand has avoidance of double taxation treaties with the following 22 countries: Austria, Belgium, Canada, China, Denmark, Finland, France, Germany, India, Indonesia, Italy, Japan, Malaysia, the Netherlands, Norway, Pakistan, Philippines, Poland, Singapore, South Korea, Sweden, and the United Kingdom. Most of these tax treaties reduce or eliminate the withholding taxes or income tax payments for nonresidents.

Free Trade Zones/Special Economic Zones

Thailand does not have any duty-free import zones per se, but projects exempted by the Board of Investment from paying duty on imported raw materials and machinery receive many of the same benefits. For administrative purposes, the Board of Investment (BOI) has divided Thailand's 73 provinces into three regions: Greater Bangkok (Bangkok and the five provinces around it); the ring of 10 provinces around Greater Bangkok; and the rest of the country. The last zone, called the Investment Promotion Zone, is where the most extensive BOI incentives are offered.

In order to exploit the natural gas resources of the Gulf of Thailand and encourage industrialization of the Eastern Seaboard, the Thai government has established two industrial estates: the Laem Chabang Industrial Estate in Chonburi Province (one and a half hours east of Bangkok) and the Map Ta Phut Industrial Estate in Rayong Province (two and a half hours east of Bangkok). Projects in these estates are eligible for the full extent of investment privileges available in the Investment Promotion Zone. In addition, as developing these industrial estates has been a priority of the Thai government, projects located there benefit from an infrastructure more sophisticated than is normally found in provincial Thailand. The government is also considering establishing a Southern Isthmus of Kra, but these plans have not yet progressed beyond the discussion phase.

APPROACHING THE MARKET

Trade and Investment Decision-Making Infrastructure

The Board of Investment (BOI) is Thailand's central investment promotion authority. Established as a result of the Investment Promotion Act of 1977, the BOI is charged with encouraging both foreign and domestic investment, particularly in sectors and locations most appropriate for Thailand's economic profile and development goals.

The BOI has a wide range of investment incentives to award potential investors whose projects meet any or all of the following criteria:

- It significantly strengthens Thailand's balance of payments position, especially through production for export.
- It supports the development of the country's resources.
- It substantially increases employment.
- It locates operations in the provinces.
- It conserves energy or replaces imported energy supplies.
- It establishes or develops industries forming the base for further stages of industrial development or those that are considered important and necessary by the government.

It is not mandatory that foreign investment in Thailand be approved by the BOI. Many foreign companies and most U.S. companies operating in Thailand do so without special BOI promoted status. Some BOI companies engage in business that is not eligible for BOI incentives. Some firms feel that the benefit of the BOI's investment incentives are outweighed by the requirements that BOI imposed regarding Thai co-ownership and export performance. In general, firms planning to use Thailand as a base for export-oriented production tend to apply for BOI promoted status more frequently than firms planning to serve mainly the domestic market.

State and Private Services

Market Research

The following companies, all located in Bangkok, offer market research, feasibility, engineering, and business consulting services in Thailand.

- Arthur Young - AMT
- Business Advisory Thailand
- CSN & Associates Co., Ltd.
- Coopers & Lybrand
- The Dharmniti Co., Ltd.
- Industrial Market Research Services
- J.P. Rooney & Associates
- Price Waterhouse
- SGV-Na Thalang & Co. (Arthur Anderson & Co.)
- Siam American Business Services Co., Ltd.
- SIAMTEC International, Ltd.
- Tara Siam Business Information Ltd.

Incorporation/Registration

The U.S.-Thai Treaty of Amity and Economic Relations of 1966 provides that U.S. citizens, businesses incorporated in the United States, and businesses incorporated in Thailand that are majority-owned by U.S. citizens shall be accorded national treatment to engage in business in Thailand. This treaty exempts U.S. investors from most foreign investment restrictions imposed by the Alien Business Decree of 1972, in return for which Thais are extended reciprocal rights to invest in the United States. Under the treaty, Thailand is permitted to apply restrictions to American investment in communications, transport, banking, the exploitation of land or other natural resources, and domestic trade in indigenous agricultural products. Aside from these areas, U.S. investors can engage in business in Thailand on the same basis as Thais.

Legal Services

The U.S.-Thai Treaty of Amity and Economic Relations does not exempt American businesses or citizens from the provisions of the Alien Occupation Law. This results in some anomalous situations; for example, an American firm or citizen can open a law firm in Thailand, but no American lawyer is permitted to practice law in Thailand. As a result, the several American-owned law firms operating in Thailand employ Thais to provide legal services. Americans and other non-Thais who are on the staff obtain work permits as "consultants."

One of the idiosyncracies of Thai law is that many minor business regulations are covered by criminal rather than civil law. In 1988, the CEO of a major American company in Thailand was sentenced to a six-month suspended jail sentence for his company's failure to meet a reporting requirement several years earlier. While this sort of problem does not arise often, it does underscore the importance of obtaining qualified legal advice when planning to invest in Thailand.

Setting Up Business Operations

Forms of Business Organization

Limited liability company. A Thai limited liability company is similar in structure to an American corporation. Promoters may form a limited company by filing a Memorandum of Association with the Ministry of Commerce. The liability of shareholders is limited to the amount of their investment, and the company is managed by a board of directors. Non-Thai citizens who will be directors of the company but who will not be working in Thailand do not require a work permit.

Generally, the minimum authorized capital of a private limited company is 100,000 baht (approximately US $4,000). When the company is registered, at least 25% of the par value of the shares of the company must be paid up.

A private limited company must have a minimum of seven promoters and seven shareholders; a public limited company must have a minimum of 15 promoters and 100 shareholders.

Branches of foreign corporations. A company incorporated under foreign laws is permitted to open a branch in Thailand. Thai branches of foreign corporations are required to maintain accounts related to activities in Thailand and transactions between the head office and the Thai branch. Under the revenue code, certain head office activities pertaining to the branch in Thailand are subject to Thai law and taxation. In order to receive an alien business license to open a branch in Thailand, a foreign corporation must agree to bring working capital equal to five million baht (approximately US $200,000) in foreign exchange into Thailand over a five-year period.

Sole traders and partnerships. There are three forms of partnership structures available: unregistered ordinary partnership, registered ordinary partnership, and limited partnership. The primary difference between the three forms of partnership is in the degree of liability attached to the partners.

Representative offices. A representative office may be established to engage in limited nontrading activities, such as identifying products, doing quality control work, or promoting business activities conducted elsewhere.

Sales Promotion, Trade Shows, and Advertising

A Western-educated marketing person will be at home in Thailand; a wide array of advertising, merchandising, public relations, and marketing firms are available. Advertising and promotion are sophisticated and Western-oriented and continue to become more so all the time. There are varied media opportunities — TV, radio, daily press, cinema, magazines, billboards, bus advertising, etc., — both in Thai and English.

Trade missions from other countries have been strongly urged to visit Thailand by the Thai government, and a large number of Thai public/private sector missions are dispatched each year to seek new outlets for Thai goods and to expand existing markets. Trade fairs have been arranged within the country, while local producers and traders have participated in those held in other countries.

Setting Up Offices

Real estate. American and other non-Thai businesses and citizens are generally not permitted to own land in Thailand, although foreign businesses are permitted to lease land. Many foreign businesses sign long-term leases and then construct buildings on the leased land. There are three instances in which a foreign company may own land: occasionally the board of investment will give a foreign company permission to own land; foreign companies are permitted to own land in government approved industrial estates; and petroleum concessionaires may own land necessary for their activities.

INVESTMENT CLIMATE

Privatization, Investment, and Dispute Settlement

In addition to the U.S.-Thai Treaty of Amity and Economic Relations of 1966, Thailand has bilateral investment agreements with the following countries: Belgium, Brunei, Canada, China, Germany, Indonesia, Korea, Luxembourg, Malaysia, Netherlands, Philippines, Singapore, and the United Kingdom. Bilateral agreements are also currently being negotiated with Austria, Bangladesh, France, Hungary, Italy, Japan, Norway, Sweden, and Switzerland.

Generally, the main objective of these treaties is to ensure the following: 1) foreign investors receive adequate compensation in the event of expropriation or nationalization, 2) the terms and conditions investors have agreed to invest remain operative for the period of investment, 3) favorable conditions exist for the repatriation of capital and profit, and 4) disputes with the government arising out of investment will be accorded fair trial by an impartial institution.

Joint Ventures and Wholly Owned Subsidiaries

Except for restrictions in the banking and insurance fields, joint venture formation in Thailand is unrestricted. It is necessary, however, to choose partners carefully. Philosophical differences in approach to business can be the root of failure.

Many Americans and other non-Thais investing in Thailand have chosen to set up a joint venture with a Thai partner, often with the Thai partner holding the majority stake. This has occurred in all fields of business and not only in those areas where foreign majority investment is prescribed by the Alien Business Decree. Many foreign investors feel the practical benefits of having a Thai partner familiar with the local economy and local regulations outweigh the cost of surrendering partial or majority stake in the venture.

Taxation and Regulatory Conditions

Company Tax

The standard rate of corporate income tax is 35% on net taxable profits. Companies registered on the Securities Exchange of Thailand (SET) pay a rate of 30%. Losses may be carried forward for five years as a deduction against net profits. Profits remitted abroad are subject to a 20% remittance tax.

Personal Income Tax

A resident of Thailand (i.e., someone who lives in Thailand 180 days or more in a given tax year) is subject to tax on income derived from sources in Thailand and on income derived from sources outside Thailand if that income is brought into the country. A nonresident is subject to tax on income derived from sources in Thailand only. Personal income tax rates in Thailand range from 5% to 55%. In general, benefits such as housing rental allowances, education allowances, and air fares for annual leave are subject to tax.

Insurance

In principle, foreign insurance firms may acquire up to 49% equity in Thai insurance firms. However, it is widely understood that no new entrants to the life insurance sector will be licensed until Thai-owned life insurance companies have increased their market shares against the American-owned market leader (which was established in 1938 and grandfathered in when restrictive regulations went into effect). This was reinforced in a November 1989 interview with a leading Thai financial journal. The Director General of the Insurance Department of the Ministry of Commerce reiterated the policy that no new entrants would be licensed.

It is also understood that no licenses will be issued for foreign or domestic firms.

No joint ventures have gotten off the ground, and there is an unofficial guideline that foreign equity holding in Thai life insurance firms should not exceed 20%.

The reinsurance market is unrestricted, and U.S. firms may participate.

FINANCING AND CAPITAL MARKETS

Banking and Other Financial Institutions

There are a total of 29 banks operating in Thailand; 15 are locally incorporated and 14 are branches of foreign banks. The commercial banks provide services mainly involving the mobilization of savings in the form of deposits and the provision of loans. All commercial banks offer foreign exchange transaction services. Mortgage business and lending have also become part of their operations.

Most banks have modernized their facilities by installing computers, microwave communication systems, automated teller machines (ATM), electronic funds transfer at point of sale (EFTPOS), etc., to provide better and faster service to customers.

There is a freeze on new foreign-owned full service banks entering Thailand, but representative (nondeposit-taking) banking offices are allowed to enter. Foreign-owned banks already in Thailand are not permitted to open branches; ATM systems are classified as branches. Foreign minority-owned financial service organizations are permitted, however, and there are several. The government has promised to open licensing for new foreign banks.

Finance companies provide four main services: short-term commercial loans; medium- and long-term loans for industrial, agricultural, and commercial undertakings; consumer credit; and housing loans. Most companies engage in all activities, but some specialize in a particular field.

Though the basic institutional framework has been established for mobilizing capital, the Thai financial market has not yet reached the point where it is a significant source of long-term capital funding. In general, foreign companies operating in Thailand provide most of their funding from offshore sources. The business finance market in Thailand is dominated by commercial banks, whose loans are essentially overdraft facilities made on a yearly or up to three-year basis.

The Securities Exchange of Thailand (SET) has grown tremendously in recent years; its average daily turnover and total capitalization (market value) more than tripling between 1987 and 1989. At year-end 1989, the SET had 175 quoted companies (including five unit trusts) and 144 quoted issues of government securities. Foreign portfolio investment in the SET reached 97.28 billion baht in 1989 (about US $3.79 billion) or approximately 13% of total turnover. In recent years, SET officials welcomed the listing of local subsidiaries of foreign-based firms. Several American companies hold majority stakes in their SET-listed Thai subsidiaries, while other U.S. firms elect only to retain significant minority shares.

Payment Modalities

In May 1990, the Thai government announced the liberalization of foreign exchange controls in line with its obligations under the IMF agreement. Under the reforms, Thailand will not place restrictions on current payment or transfers for current international transactions, it will refrain from engaging in discriminatory currency arrangements or multiple currency practices, and it will accept convertibility of foreign-held balances.

LICENSING, PATENTS, AND TRADEMARKS

Trademark, Patent, and Copyright Protection

Enhanced trademark protection was expected by the end of 1989; a new trademark law was drafted and presented to the Parliament in September 1989.

Thailand enacted a patent law in 1979; however, pharmaceuticals, food products, and agricultural machinery are excluded from patent coverage. After considerable internal debate of U.S. requests that patent protection be allowed, the Thai government reaffirmed its position that no changes are possible at this time, although there are indications that such changes could come within a few years. The government argues that Thailand is a developing country whose people cannot afford to pay Western prices for patented medicines. Negotiating efforts based on section 301 of the 1988 Trade Act could bring changes. A new patent law is not expected until 1992 or 1993 at the earliest.

Thailand's patent law requires that the patent holder work the patent in Thailand to obtain protection against products believed to be infringing the patent. How courts interpret "working the patent" varies from case to case. Exporting and selling through an agent have been interpreted as satisfying this requirement.

During the 1986-1987 GSP General Review, Thailand promised the United States it would correct the series of past administrative lapses which resulted in the United States being deprived of direct copyright protection in Thailand. A copyright law was submitted to Parliament and passed in May 1987, but the Parliament was dissolved, new elections were called, and the legislation had to begin the process again.

Since the United States joined the Berne Convention in March 1989, much of the pressure on Thailand has been relieved. The current focus of efforts to protect U.S. copyrights in Thailand is to use the Thai legal system to go after the major copyright violators. U.S. accession to the Berne Convention was the mechanism by which Thailand fulfilled its commitment to protect U.S. copyrighted works.

The Thai government has also provided assurance that "pre-existing" U.S. works still under protection in the United States will now be protected under Thai law. And, although Thailand's copyright law does not provide explicit protection for computer software, the highly respected Thai Juridical Council gave an advisory opinion in 1984 that software is protected by the Thai copyright law. The governments of both Thailand and the United States have stated a willingness to await a Thai court test of the Juridical Council's advisory opinion on computer software.

VISITING AND LOCATING

General Travel Checklist

Visas

A passport or internationally recognized travel document valid beyond the duration of one's expected stay in Thailand is required. Foreign nationals of many countries can obtain a 15-day transit visa upon arrival if evidence of an onward ticket is produced. A 60-day tourist visa can be obtained from Thai embassies and consulates abroad. Holders of these visas are reminded that visa expiry dates should be strictly observed. In emergency situations, such as illness, requests for an extension of stay (together with supporting evidence) must be made to the Immigration Division prior to the visa's expiration date.

Currency

The baht is the Thai unit of currency. Paper denominations come in 500, 100, 100, 50, 20 and 10 baht notes; coins come in 5, 2, 1, 0.5, and 0.25 baht values. The baht's value is managed by the Bank of Thailand's Exchange Equalization Fund and fluctuates according to the movements of a basket of Thailand's major trading partners' currencies. In practice, the baht is closely aligned with the U.S. dollar. All major credit cards and traveler's checks are widely accepted in hotels, shops, and most restaurants.

Visitors are allowed to bring an unlimited amount of foreign currency into the country but should declare the amount to the Customs officers at the time of entry since the visitor cannot take out more foreign currency than was declared on arrival. Careful attention should be paid to reading and accurately completing the Customs Declaration form issued to all visitors upon arrival.

Getting Around

Thailand has a well-developed national transportation system including an excellent national highway network, rail services to all regions, and the domestic airline network, which connects most provincial centers with Bangkok.

In Bangkok, the business visitor who does not speak Thai and is not familiar with the city is advised to use hotel taxis or hire cars with drivers. Public taxis are plentiful and cheaper, but meters are not used and fares should be negotiated before getting into the taxi.

Accommodations and Housing

Bangkok offers some of the world's greatest hotels, nearly two dozen deluxe first-class hotels and a wide range of more economical accommodations. Rooms suitable for the business visitor range from US $50 and up plus 10% service charge and 11% tax.

Electricity Supply

The local electric power operates on 220 volts, 50 hertz.

Telecom, Postal, and Courier Services

International telephone, telex, and telegraph facilities are available in urban areas throughout the country. International direct dialing to most countries is available at most first-class hotels. Otherwise, international calls must be made through the exchange operator which takes a little longer.

Business Cards

Bring a plentiful supply of business cards and use them with every new business contact.

Business Hours

Business hours, Monday through Friday, start at 8:30 a.m. to 12:00 p.m. and then reopen from 1:00 p.m. to 5:30 p.m. Some offices are open on Saturday from 8:30 a.m. to 12:00 p.m. Banking hours are 8:30 a.m. to 3:00 p.m. on Monday through Friday. Government office hours begin at 8:30 a.m. to 12:00 p.m. and reopen from 1:00 p.m. to 4:30 p.m. on a five-day week.

Tipping

It is customary to tip hotel porters but not taxi-drivers, as the negotiated rate is inclusive. Tipping in restaurants is optional.

What to Wear

Average temperature is 27.6 degrees celsius (81.7 degrees fahrenheit) ranging from a high of 32.5 degrees celsius (90.5 degrees fahrenheit) in April to a low of 23.7 degrees celsius (74.7 degrees fahrenheit) in January. Three distinct seasons exist: from March to May it's very hot; from June to October it's very hot, very humid, and sometimes very wet; and from November to January, officially the "cool" season, it's enjoyable.

Light clothing is worn all year. For foreigners, business suits are the norm, although safari suits are popular and acceptable as business attire depending on the working environment. Only a very few restaurants offering Western cuisine in the best hotels require a coat and tie for dinner.

Health Care

Although Bangkok's public water supply is safe, most foreign visitors, without the benefit of acclimatization, prefer to drink bottled water. Medical facilities including doctors, dentists, and hospitals in Bangkok are regarded as being the best in

Southeast Asia. The larger public and private hospitals offer the latest in medical technology and internationally qualified specialists. Most first-class hotels have a house doctor or nurse on call.

Hospitals are available for routine treatment. Mosquitoes are plentiful, but malaria is not a problem in Bangkok. Hepatitis is fairly common in Thailand. Avoid tap water, raw milk, ice cream, uncooked meats, and unwashed raw fruits and vegetables.

The Media

There is a wide variety of media in both Thai and English, including television, radio, daily press, cinema, magazines, billboards, bus advertising, etc.

Availability of Foreign Products

Thailand has an astonishing variety of imported products on display in stores everywhere. Overall, the duty weight in imported goods in Thailand averages 35%, high by U.S. standards but not by Asian standards.

Shopping

Bangkok is a veritable "gold mine" for shoppers. Bargaining is common and part of the fun, except in the department stores which have proliferated in recent years. Popular items at internationally competitive prices include Thai silk, gems and jewelry, all types of handicrafts, clothing, and leather goods.

Dining Out

Thailand is a gourmet's paradise. Dining in hotel restaurants is more expensive than eating out at one of the thousands of Thai and Chinese restaurants scattered throughout Bangkok.

Entertainment

With over 2.5 million tourists visiting the country each year, Thailand is famous for its wide range of cultural, entertainment, and sporting facilities. If your trip includes a weekend, it is suggested that you visit the international beach resort of Pattaya, the quieter resorts of Cha-am, Phuket, and Hua Hin, or the hills of Chiangmai in the north. Horse racing, golfing, sailing, jungle trekking, and river rafting are all available.

Sightseeing and Tourist Information

Check with your hotel or the Tourism Authority of Thailand (Tel: 282-1143-9).

The Short-Term Business Visitor

Airlines Serving

Bangkok is one of the main airline connection points in Asia. A complete listing of the fifty airlines maintaining office in Bangkok may be found in the English edition of the Bangkok Telephone Directory's Yellow Pages.

Limousine

The Bangkok Yellow Pages list local and international automobile rental companies. Visitors are advised to shop around since most companies offer different conditions. Self-drive and chauffeur-driven automobiles are widely available.

The Expatriate

Immigration and Work Permits

Foreign nationals wishing to work in Thailand must hold a nonimmigrant visa and a work permit, the latter being specific to both an individual and the position held in a firm. Work permits are issued by the Labor Department and must be obtained before starting work. Foreigners considering investing in Thailand or working for a company promoted by the Board of Investment should contact the Board's Investment Services Center to receive special assistance with visas and work permits.

American citizens are permitted to enter Thailand without a visa for stays of up to 14 days. In order to apply for a work permit, which must be obtained in Thailand, a foreigner must enter Thailand on a nonimmigrant visa. Nonimmigrant visas are issued at Thai embassies and consulates for a stay of three months or, for foreigners with well-defined work or business plans, for a stay of one year. Issuance of the three-month visa is usually completed within two or three days; the one-year visa requires approval from the Immigration Department in Bangkok.

Upon obtaining a work permit, a holder of a three-month visa may apply for a one-year visa. One-year visas can generally be extended on a yearly basis. Foreigners who hold nonimmigrant visas and have lived in Thailand for at least two years may apply for permanent residence in Thailand if they meet strict criteria regarding investment in Thailand or professional skills.

THAILAND

KEY CONTACTS

American Embassy Contacts

American Embassy Bangkok
95 Wireless Road
APO San Francisco 96346
   Tel: 66/2-252-5040
   Fax: 66/2-255-2915

Commercial Office
"R" Fl., Kian Gwan Bldg.
140 Wireless Road
   Tel: 66/2-253-4920/2
   Fax: 66/2-254-2990

Ambassador:	David F. Lambertson
Deputy Chief of Mission:	Victor L. Tomseth
Political Section:	Ralph L. Boyce
Economic Section:	Robert B. Duncan
Commercial Section:	Herbert A. Cochran
Labor Officer:	R. Niels Marquardt
Consul (Consular Section):	David L. Lyon
Administrative Section:	Gerald E. Manderscheid
Regional Security Officer:	William H. O'Rouke
Agricultural Section:	Weyland Beeghly
Agency for International Development:	John R. Erikkson
Public Affairs Officer:	Donna Marie Oglesby
Narcotics Assistance Unit:	Albert L. Bryant
Refugee Coordinator:	Bruce A. Beardsley
Customs Service:	James L. Cable
Immigration and Naturalization Officer:	James B. Foster
Office of the Defense Attache:	Col. Vernon D. Ellis, U.S.A.F.
Joint U.S. Military Advisory Group:	Bg. Peter W. Lash, U.S.A.

Key Contacts in the Public and Private Sector

Government and Quasi-Governmental

Ministry of Commerce:

Foreign Trade Dept.
  Tel: 223-1481-5
  Telex: 72277 DEPFORT TH

Commercial Registration Dept.
  Tel: 222-0858

Ministry of Finance:

Customs Dept.
  Tel: 249-0431-40

Revenue Dept.
  Tel: 281-5777

Ministry of Interior:

Immigration Division
  Tel: 286-4231

Ministry of Industry:

Industrial Promotion Dept.
  Tel: 246-0033

Board of Investment:

Bangkok
  Tel: 270-1400/270-1410
  Telex: 72435 BINVEST TH

Frankfurt
  Tel: 0611-281091-2
  Telex: 4189399TTICD

New York
  Tel: 212-466-1745/6
  Telex: 645690 THAICOM NYK

Sydney
Tel: 278905-6
Telex: THAITC AA 23467
Tokyo
Tel: 03-5821-086
Telex: 2426991 BOITYO

Bank of Thailand

Tel: 282-3322
Telex: 72012 BNKCHAT TH

Bank for Agriculture and Agricultural Cooperatives

Tel: 282-5181-90

Department of Export Promotion:

Head Office:
22/77 Rachadapisek Road
Bangkok 10900
Thailand
Tel: 511-5066-77/513-1909
Telex: 82354 DEPEP TH/81009 DEPEP TH
Fax: 662-512-1079

Chamber of Commerce

American
Tel: 251-1605
Fax: 253-9628

Australian
Tel: 233-4476
Telex: 82505 PFIZER TH

British
Tel: 234-2180
Fax: 233-0518

Chinese
Tel: 211-2365
Telex: 87265 KINSON TH
Fax: 212-1639

French
Tel: 251-9386
Telex: 21005 FTCC TH

German
Tel: 236-2396
Telex: 82836 GTCC TH

Indian
Tel: 286-1961

Italian
Tel: 247-1558
Telex: 84070 TURISMO TH
Fax: 246-3993

Japanese
Tel: 256-9170

Professional and Trade Associations

Federation of Thai Industries (FTI) is the foremost organization for Thai manufacturers:

Tel: 280-0951
Telex: 72202 INDUSTI TH

With the FTI, two other powerful organizations comprise the Joint Standing Committee on Commerce, Industry and Banking which is Thailand's constituent member in the ASEAN-CCI, Southeast Asia's most influential private sector body. The other two organizations are:

Board of Trade of Thailand
Tel: 222-9031
Telex: 84309 BOT TH

Thai Bankers' Association
Tel: 234-1818
Telex: 21341 NABANK TH

INFORMATION
RESOURCES

U.S. DEPARTMENT OF COMMERCE

1. International Trade Administration

   A. Deputy Assistant Secretary — East Asia and the Pacific
      14th & Constitution Avenue, NW
      Room 3820
      Washington, DC 20230
         Tel: 202/377-5251 or 202/377-2000

   B. Country Desk Officers (Locator: 202/377-2000)

ASEAN	George Paine	202/377-3875
Hong Kong	Jenelle Matheson	202/377-2462
Indonesia	Don Ryan	202/377-3875
Japan	Maureen Smith	202/377-4527
Korea	Dan Duvall	202/377-4958
Malaysia	Jeff Hardee	202/377-3875
Singapore	Jeff Hardee	202/377-3875
Taiwan	Laurie Hurtado	202/377-4957
Thailand	Linda Droker	202/377-3875

   C. Office of Telecommunications
      Richard Paddock, Director for Major Projects
         Tel: 202/377-1304

2. National Telecommunications and Information Administration
   Jack Gleason, Director
      Tel: 202/377-1304

3. Office of Technology Policy Assessment
   William Clements, Director
      Tel: 202/377-4188

4. Bureau of Export Administration
   Joe Westlake, Director
      Tel: 202/377-0730

5. Office of Domestic Service
   Export Counseling Center: Room 10066
   (Export counseling and marketing assistance) 202/377-3181

6. Export Promotion Services
   Office of Information Product Development & Distribution:
   P.O. Box 14207
   Washington, DC 20044
   (Reports on markets and trade leads)...202/377-2432

   Office of Marketing Programs
   (Trade shows and trade missions)...202/377-4231

   Information on *Commercial News USA* and other
   commerce export-related publications.....................................202/377-5367

7. Trade Development — Product Service Specialists:

   Aerospace: Room 6877...202/377-8228
   Automotive Affairs and Consumer Goods: Room 4324 ....202/377-0823
   Basic Industries: Room 4045 ....202/377-0614
   Capital Goods & Construction: Room 2001B 202/377-5023
   Export Trading Company Affairs: Room 5618 ....202/377-5131
   International Major Projects: Room 2007 ....202/377-5225
   Science & Electronics: Room 1001A 202/377-4466
   Services: Room 1128 ....202/377-5261
   Textiles & Apparel: Room 3100..202/377-4466
   Trade Information & Analysis: Room 3814B 202/377-1316

8. Trade Administration: Office of Export Administration

   Exporter's Service Staff: (Export Licensing, controls, etc.)
   Room 1099 ....

U.S. Department of Treasury

U.S. Department of Treasury
15th & Pennsylvania Avenue, NW
Washington, DC 20220

U.S. Customs Strategic Investigation Division 202/566-9464
   (Exodus Command Center)

Office of The United States Trade Representative

Winder Building
600 17th Street, NW
Washington, DC 20506

General Counsel 202/395-3150
Private Sector Liaison 202/395-6120
Agriculture Affairs & Commodity Policy 202/395-6127
The Americas Trade Policy 202/395-6135
East-West & Non-Market Economies 202/395-4543
Europe & Japan 202/395-4620
General Agreement on Tariff and Trade (GATT) 202/395-6843
Industrial & Energy Trade Policy 202/395-7320
Investment Policy 202/395-3510
Pacific, Asia, Africa & North-South Trade Policy 202/395-3430

Small Business Administration (SBA)

All export programs administered through SBA are available through SBA field offices. More information about the programs can be obtained through:

Small Business Administration (SBA) 202/653-7794
Office of International Trade
1441 L Street, NW
Washington, DC 20416

U.S. Trade & Development Program (TDP)

The Trade and Development Program (TDP), is an independent U.S. government agency of the International Development Cooperation Agency (IDCA), which promotes economic development in middle income and developing countries by funding feasibility studies and other project planning services. In Eastern Europe, TDP assists U.S. firms by identifying major development projects which offer large export potential and by funding U.S. private sector involvement in project planning. This, in turn, helps position U.S. firms for following on contracts when these projects are implemented.

TDP currently has activities in Hong Kong, Indonesia, Korea, Malaysia, the Pacific Islands, the Philippines, Singapore, Taiwan, and Thailand.

TDP activities cover a wide range of sectors of high priority to host governments and international development efforts. Additionally, TDP has statutory authority to facilitate access to natural resources of interest to the United States. U.S. technological expertise can help accelerate the development process on all these sectors. They include, but are not limited to, telecommunications, industry, energy development, transportation, educational technology, minerals development, and waste treatment.

Other areas of expressed interest which TDP will pursue, subject to availability of funds, include power sector modernization, transportation, and selected industrial priorities.

For more information on the TDP program in Eastern Europe, inquiries may be addressed to Fred Eberhart, Regional Director for Asia-Pacific, SA-16, Room 309, Washington, D.C. 20523-1602, Tel: 703/875-4357; Fax: 703/875-4009.

Overseas Private Investment Corporation (OPIC)

The Overseas Private Investment Corporation (OPIC) is a self-sustaining U.S. government agency whose purpose is to promote economic growth in developing countries by encouraging U.S. private investment in those nations.

OPIC's key programs are its loan guarantees, direct loans, and political risk insurance.

For additional information on OPIC programs in Eastern Europe, address your inquiries to James V. Hall, Director of Public Affairs, Telephone: 202/457-7093; Fax: 202/223-3514.

Other Sources of Information

East Asian Business Intelligence

Excellent biweekly newsletter of business-oriented news, with early alerts on impending procurements and projects.

William C. Hearn, Editor and Publisher
International Executive Reports, Ltd.
717 D Street, NW #300
Washington, DC 20004-2807
   Tel: 202/628-6900
   Fax: 202/628-6618
   Telex: 440462 MEER UI

Embassies and Commercial Offices in the United States

Ambassador Krit Garnjana-Goonchorn
Embassy of Thailand
2300 Kalorama Road, NW
Washington, DC 20008
 Tel: 202/483-7200

Ambassador S.R. Nathan
Embassy of Singapore
182 R Street, NW
Washington, DC 20009
 Tel: 202/667-7555
 Fax: 202/265-7915

Commercial Office
 Tel: 213/617-7358

Ambassador Abdul Rachman Ramly
Embassy of Indonesia
2020 Massachusetts Avenue, NW
Washington, DC 20036
 Tel: 202/775-5200

Commercial Office
2020 Massachusetts Avenue, NW
Washington, DC 20036
 Tel: 202/775-5350

Ambassador A.R. Ahmad Fuzi
Embassy of Malaysia
2401 Massachusetts Avenue, NW
Washington, DC 20008
 Tel: 202/328-2700
 Fax: 202/483-7661

Commercial Office
2407 California Street, NW
Washington, DC 20008
 Tel: 202/328-2783
 Fax: 202/332-8914

Ambassador Emmanuel Pelaez
Embassy of the Philippines
1617 Massachusetts Avenue, NW
Washington, DC 20036
 Tel: 202/483-1414
 Fax: 202/328-7614

Commercial Office
1617 Massachusetts Avenue, NW
Washington, DC 20036
 Tel: 202/387-2810
 Fax: 202/332-2320

Ambassador Hong-Choo Hyun
Embassy of Korea
2370 Massachusetts Avenue, NW
Washington, DC 20008
 Tel: 202/939-5600

Commercial Office
2320 Massachusetts Avenue, NW
Washington, DC 20008
 Tel: 202/939-5642
 Fax: 202/797-0595

Embassy of Hong Kong
1233 20th Street, NW
Suite 504
Washington, DC 20036
 Tel: 202/331-8947
 Fax: (202) 331-8958

Commercial Office
Trade Development Council
219 East 42d Street
New York, NY 10017
    Tel: 212/839-8688
    Fax: 212/383-8941

TRADE SHOWS AND CONFERENCES

TRADE SHOWS AND CONFERENCES — 1990 - 1992

Date	Location	Description
1990		
January 14-17	Honolulu	PTC 90 — Pacific Telecom Council. [PTC]
March 6-9	Sydney	Communications 90/Office Technology 90. Australian Exhibition Svcs. Pty. Ltd. [AES]
March 20-24	Jakarta	International Computer & Business Equipment Exhibition, Indonesia.
March 27-29	Tokyo	Super Computing Japan 90.
April 10-14	Jakarta	Intertelec, Indonesia.
April 18-21	Tokyo	Communications Tokyo 90 — Purpose was to display and demonstrate the latest state-of-the-art telecom equipment and systems. Over 85,000 attended in 1989. [EJK]
April 19-27	PacRim	U.S. Department of Commerce Trade Mission to Philippines, Indonesia and Thailand. [USDOC]
May 17-20	Kuala Lumpur	ASIA TELECOMS, Malaysia.
May 29-June 1	Singapore	InfotechAsia 90. [K&A]
May 29-June 1	Singapore	Communicasia 90. [K&A]
May 29-June 1	Singapore	BroadcastAsia 90. [K&A]
August 4-7	Bangkok	AsiaComm 90, Thailand. Third International Telecom Technology Trade Exhibit and Seminar. [TRADEX]
August 12-15	Melbourne	Communications 90/Office Technology 90. Australian Exhibition Svcs. Pty. Ltd. [AES]
September 6-9	Bangkok	Infomatic + Telematic 90, Thailand.
September 11-15	Manila	Phil Telecom 90, Philippines. [SHK]

AES = Australian Exhibition Service Pty. Ltd.
HANN = Hannover Fairs
PTC = Pacific Telecom Council
TRADEX = TRADEX

EJK = EJ Krause
K&A = Kallman & Associates
SHK = SHK International
USDOC = U.S. Department of Commerce

Date	Location	Description
		1990
September 17-20	Kuala Lampur	ICIT90 — International Conference on Information Technology, held in conjunction with trade exhibit. Contact: ICIT90 Secretariat, Malaysian National Computer Confederation, 46A Jalan SS 2/66, 47300 Petaling Jaya, SDelangor Darul Ehsan, Malaysia. Tel: 03-775-1576, 03-776-5160. Telex: MA 33735 DEMSB. Fax: 03-774-7026.
September 25-27	Hong Kong	Mil Comp 90.
September 25-28	Hong Kong	CENIT ASIA 90. [HANN]
November 2-5	Bangkok	Office + Telematic 90, Thailand.
November 8-13	Beijing	EXPO COMM China 90. [EJK]
November 28- December 1	Bangkok	Communications Thailand 90.
December 6-9	Hong Kong	Comtel Asia 90.
		1991
September	Beijing	TeleComp China 91 — Hosted by the China Council for the Promotion of International Trade and China International Exhibition Centre. Covers office automation and computers. About 100 exhibitors from 12 countries participated in 1989.

1992

Pacific Telecom Council PTC '92
1100 University Avenue #308
Honolulu, HI 96826-1508
  Tel: 808/941-3789
  Fax: 808/944-4874

Held annually in January, this is the key trade show for the telecom sector in the Pacific Rim.

AES = Australian Exhibition Service Pty. Ltd.
HANN = Hannover Fairs
PTC = Pacific Telecom Council
TRADEX = TRADEX

EJK = EJ Krause
K&A = Kallman & Associates
SHK = SHK International
USDOC = U.S. Department of Commerce

Date	Location	Description

1992

CommTel International Conference '92
c/o BDG Management Limited
705 East Town Building # 705
41 Lockhart Road
Hong Kong
  Tel: 852-528-6136
  Fax: 852-865-1528

This is the third annual conference organized by the Hong Kong Telecom Association and the Hong Kong Telecom Users Group.

Exhibitor Key

AES	Australian Exhibition Services Pty. Ltd. Tel: 011/61-3-267-4500
EJK	EJ Krause. Bethesda, MD, USA. Tel: 301/986-7800 Fax: 301/986-4538
HANN	Hannover Fairs. Princeton, NJ, USA. Tel: 609/987-1202
K&A	Kallman & Associates. New Jersey, USA. Tel: 201/652-7070
PTC	Pacific Telecom Council. Honolulu, HI, USA. Tel: 808/941-3789
SHK	SHK International. Fax: 852-5-838-0639
TRADEX	TRADEX Tel: 011/66-12-279-5455
USDOC	U.S. Department of Commerce. Washington, DC, USA. Tel: 202/377-2000

APPENDIX

Table A-1: Top Pacific Rim Markets for U.S. Domestic and Foreign Merchandise Exports (1989)

Country	$Billions
Japan	44.6
South Korea	13.5
Taiwan	11.3
Singapore	7.4
Hong Kong	6.3
Malaysia	2.9

Source: U.S. Department of Commerce.

Table A-2: 1990 Global Price Comparisons* in Selected Asian/Pacific Locations

Locations	Lunch	Man's Shirt	Woman's Blouse	Milk of Magnesia	Razor Blade	Toothpaste
Auckland	$10.77	$35.45	$48.53	$4.86	$1.69	$2.28
Bangkok	7.16	18.04	26.38	1.06	1.26	1.66
Guangzhou	6.02	14.71	8.19	NA	3.07	2.24
Kuala Lumpur	6.76	19.28	29.66	NA	1.23	2.02
Manila	6.47	16.11	19.09	7.41	1.55	2.02
Tokyo	19.01	49.24	80.94	7.67	2.65	4.38

* The goods and services above represent average prices in the countries shows in U.S. dollars and include sales tax and value-added tax where appropriate.

Source: Runzheimer International, *Reports on Travel Management* (Monthly), Northbrook, IL 60062. (Tel: 414/534-3121).

Table A-3: Pacific Rim Comparative Profiles (May 1990)

	GDP ($ Million, 1987)	GDP Growth Rate (Percentage/Year, 1980-87)	Manufactures as Percentage of GDP (1987)	Unemployment Rate (1988)	Average Hourly Wage Rate for Production of Workers (1988)	Literacy Rate (Percentage of Population 1988)
Hong Kong	36,530	5.8	22%	1.4%	$2.43	88%
Indonesia	69,670	3.6	14%	2.2%	$1.30	74%
Japan	2,374,000	3.8	32%	2.6%	$13.14	99%
Malaysia	31,320	4.5	25%	8.1%	$0.46	76%
Philippines	34,580	-0.7	25%	8.5%	$0.40	86%
Singapore	19,900	5.4	29%	3.4%	$2.67	87%
South Korea	121,310	8.6	30%	2.5%	$2.46	96%
Taiwan	91,330	8.3	44%	1.7%	$2.71	92%
Thailand	48,200	5.6	24%	3.5%	$1.10	91%

Source: Central Intelligence Agency. *The World Factbook 1990*, Washington, DC 20505 (Tel: 703/351-2053).

Table A-4: Pacific Rim Economic Indicators

Country	Population 1988 (Millions)	Per Capita GNP 1988 (U.S.$)	Inflation (CPI Percentage Change) (U.S.$) 1989
Hong Kong	5.6	9,230.00	10.0
Indonesia	175.0	430.00	6.5
Japan	54.0	1,000.00	6.0
Korea	42.5	3,530.00	6.5
Malaysia	16.9	1,870.00	3.5
Philippines	60.0	630.00	11.0
Singapore	2.6	9,100.00	2.6
Thailand	19.9	6,333.00	6.5

Source: The World Bank, *Social Indicators of Development*, 1989, (1818 H Street, NW, Washington, DC 20433).

Table A-5: Pacific Rim Standard of Living Indicators (1989)

Country	Population per Telephone	Population per Car	Population per Physician	Calories per Person	Life Expectancy	Infant Mortality per 1,000
Hong Kong	2	34	1,075	2,859	76	8
Indonesia	226	167	9,464	2,579	60	71
Japan	2	4	663	2,864	78	6
Korea	4	74	1,666	2,907	69	25
Malaysia	11	11	1,935	2,730	69	24
Philippines	66	155	6,700	2,372	63	45
Singapore	2	11	1,309	2,840	72	9
Thailand	52	74	6,294	2,331	66	39

Source: The World Bank, *Social Indicators of Development*, 1989, (1818 H Street, NW, Washington, DC 20433).

Table A-6: Pacific Rim Price Comparisons

(As of January 4, 1991)

Location	Exchange U.S. $ =	Snack (8 oz. Potato Chips)	Single Dinner	Fast Food (Burger Soft Drink, and Fries)	Beer (Six-Pack)	Alka Seltzer (36 Tabs)	Service to Launder Shirt	Tennis Balls (Three)	Single Lodging Business Class
Hong Kong	7.79	2.05	34.07	2.48	2.62	4.73	1.58	3.97	217.23
Singapore	1.75	2.10	28.00	3.10	9.47	5.88	2.01	5.66	159.86
Tokyo, Japan	134.80	2.65	61.94	5.39	11.44	NA	3.18	3.18	228.07

(As of January 28, 1991)

Location	Exchange U.S. $ =	Yogurt (8 oz.)	Breakfast	Cigarettes (One Carton)	Wine (750 ml.)	Woman's Cut and Dry	Man's Haircut	Single Lodging Business Class
Seoul, South Korea	716.40	1.02	13.31	12.93	5.47	29.09	11.42	178.62
Taipei, Taiwan	27.14	0.99	14.29	12.35	10.76	17.54	13.58	188.39

(As of April 18, 1991)

Location	Exchange U.S. $ =	Business Lunch for Two	Aspirin (100 Tablets)	Mineral Water (32 oz.)	Man's Haircut	Tooth-paste (3.5 oz.)	Hotel Three Star	Taxi Ride (Two Kilometers)	State Department per Diem	ORC per Diem	Cab Ride (Airport to City Center)
Jakarta, Indonesia	1,927.13	16.03	2.47	0.34	11.68	1.75	185.10	0.73	167.00	253.91	20.00
Kuala Lumpur, Malaysia	2.74	13.88	4.38	0.72	14.07	1.10	140.76	0.55	108.00	223.60	5.85

Source: Runzheimer International, *Reports on Travel Management* (Monthly), Northbrook, IL 60062 (Tel: 414/534-3121).

Table A-7: Wholesale Industries in Japan

Number of Wholesale Establishments	413,016 (1985)	
Number of Employees	3,998,000 (1985)	
	NA (1988)	
Number of Employees per Establishment	9.7 (1985)	
Population per Wholesale Employee	30.3 (1985)	
	NA (1988)	
Annual Sales (millions of dollars)	$1,795,468 (1985)	Y238.54=$1.00
	$3,502,154 (1988)	Y128.15=$1.00
Annual Sales per Establishment	$4,347,380 (1985)	Y238.54=$1.00
Annual Sales per Employee	$449,092 (1985)	Y238.54=$1.00
	NA (1988)	
Wholesale/Retail Turnover Ratio	4.21 (1985)	
	NA (1988)	

Source: Embassy of Japan (Washington).

Table A-8: Japanese Economic Indicators (Percentage Change from Previous Year Unless Otherwise Indicated)

	1987	1988	January-June 1988	January-June 1989	April 1989	May 1989	June 1989
Discount Rate (end of period)	2.5%	2.5%	2.5%	3.25%	2.5%	3.25%	3.25%
Outstanding Money Supply	10.4%	11.2%	11.7%	10.0%*	10.2%	9.4%	9.4%*
Industrial Production	3.4%	9.5%	10.6%	7.4%*	6.1%	7.4%	7.3%*
Manufacturing Operating Rate	0.1%	5.9%	6.4%	NA	3.1%	3.9%	NA
Number of Bankruptcies	-27.6%	-20.0%	-20.4%	-26.2%	-29.1%	-25.4%	-23.2%
Residential Construction Starts	22.7%	0.6%	8.8%	-2.4%	4.4%	-0.4%	-2.1%
Job Openings to Applications (ratio)	0.7	1.02	0.94	120.0%	116.0%	127.0%	1.34
Nominal Wages	1.9%	3.8%	3.1%	4.6%*	4.0%	4.0%	6.8%*
Labor Productivity	5.8%	11.5%	12.5%**	10.1%**	NA	NA	NA
Wholesale Prices	-3.7%	-1.0%	-0.8%	1.7%	2.5%	3.4%	3.7%
Consumer Prices	0.1%	0.7%	0.5%	1.9%	2.4%	2.9%	3.0%
Yen-Based Export Prices	-5.1%	-2.2%	-3.8%	4.0%	3.5%	5.7%	7.5%
Yen-Based Import Prices	-8.3%	-4.6%	-3.4%	5.0%	6.8%	10.6%	10.7%

* Preliminary

** January-March of each year only.

Source: Embassy of Japan (Washington).

Table A-9: Japanese Trade and Payments Data (In Millions of Dollars Unless Otherwise Indicated)

	1987	1988	January-June 1988	January-June 1989	April 1989	May 1989	June 1989
Japan's Balance of Payments							
Trade Balance	$96,386	$95,012	$43,469	$40,930 *	$8,123 *	$5,058 *	$6,438 *
Exports (f.o.b.)	$224,605	$259,765	$122,904	$133,338 *	$22,796 *	$21,325 *	$22,272 *
Imports (f.o.b.)	$128,219	$164,753	$79,435	$92,408 *	$14,673 *	$16,267 *	$15,834 *
Current Account Balance	$87,015	$79,631	$36,988	$30,051 *	$6,483 *	$3,388 *	$4,116 *
Long-Term Capital (net)	($136,532)	($130,930)	($51,698)	$35,708 *	($16,241) *	($12,252) *	($1,603) *
Overall Balance	($29,545)	($28,982)	($11,009)	($2,926)	($23,232)	($12,456)	$8,808
International ...s (end c. period)	$81,749	$97,662	$87,700	$89,462	$100,361	$95,694	$89,462
Japan's Customs Clearance Trade							
Trade Balance	$79,706	$77,563	$33,692	$33,469 *	$7,318	$3,761	$5,291 *
Exports (f.o.b.)	$229,221	$264,917	$125,457	$135,833 *	$23,225	$21,707	$22,654 *
Cars	$35,693	$38,671	$18,787	$19,803 *	$3,738	$2,940	$3,037 *
Steel	$12,610	$15,322	$7,034	$7,597 *	$1,282	$1,238	$1,265 *
Imports (c.i.f.)	$149,515	$187,354	$91,765	$102,364 *	$15,908	$17,946	$17,363 *
Crude Oil	$20,663	$18,852	$10,522	$10,276 *	$1,803	$1,775	$1,550 *
Manufactured Products	$65,961	$91,838	$44,144	$51,020 *	$8,040	$8,728	$8,665 *

* Preliminary

Source: Embassy of Japan (Washington).

Table A-9: Japanese Trade and Payments Data (Continued)

	1987	1988	January-June 1988	January-June 1989	April 1989	May 1989	June 1989
Japan-U.S. Trade							
Trade Balance	$52,090	$47,597	$20,921	$22,108 *	$4,557	$2,754	$3,635 *
Exports (f.o.b.)	$83,580	$89,634	$41,469	$45,724 *	$7,924	$7,140	$7,932 *
Imports (c.i.f.)	$31,491	$42,037	$20,549	$23,616 *	$3,366	$4,387	$4,297 *
Yen-Dollar Exchange Rate							
(Average for Period)	Y144.64	Y128.15	Y126.81	Y133.26	Y132.08	Y138.35	Y143.79
U.S. Trade							
Trade Balance	($152,119)	($118,526)	($56,595)	($50,041)*	($6,818)	($9,625)	($9,122)*
Exports (f.a.s.)	$254,122	$322,426	$158,543	$182,186 *	$31,367	$31,271	$31,159 *
Imports (Customs)	$406,241	$440,952	$215,138	$232,227 *	$38,185	$40,896	$40,281 *
U.S.-Japan Trade							
Trade Balance	($56,326)	($52,070)	($24,121)	($24,521)*	($3,893)	($4,281)	($3,940) *
Exports (f.a.s.)	$28,249	$37,732	$18,228	$21,605 *	$3,637	$3,603	$3,966 *
Imports (Customs)	$84,575	$89,802	$42,350	$46,126 *	$7,530	$7,884	$7,907 *

* Preliminary

Source: Embassy of Japan (Washington).

Table A-10: Japan: Trends in Direct Investment Overseas (US$ Millions)

	1982	1983	1984	1985	1986	1987	1988
North America	2,905	2,701	3,544	5,495	10,440	15,537	22,328
Europe	876	990	1,937	1,930	3,469	6,576	9,116
Asia	1,385	1,847	1,628	1,435	2,327	4,868	5,569
Latin America	1,503	1,878	2,290	2,616	4,737	4,816	6,428
Others	1,034	729	756	741	1,346	1,747	3,581
Total	7,703	8,145	10,155	12,217	22,320	33,364	47,022

Source: Minister of Finance (1990).

Table A-11: Japan: Import Penetration Ratio (Based on Quantity)

	1980	1986	1987	1988
Steel Pipes	0.6	3.8	5.2	8.1
Steel, Ores	0.9	2.8	7.6	12.7
Photo Films	29.4	36.8	39.5	39.3
Lathes	20.5	30.4	40.2	43.5
Electronic Calculators	12.9	44.7	49.0	42.8
Portable Radios	38.8	39.9	55.7	60.6
Radios/Cassette Tape Recorders	4.6	15.3	47.5	44.7
Semiconductors	22.2	21.2	25.3	28.3
Motor Vehicles	1.6	2.2	3.1	3.7
35mm Cameras	7.7	19.4	46.6	48.2

Source: American Embassy, Tokyo (1990).

Table A-12: Economic Profile of Korea (1990)

Real GNP Growth	7.3%
Overall Consumption	8.0%
Fixed Investment	13.3%
Investment in Plant and Equipment	11.4%
Investment in Construction	14.9%
Current Account Deficit (Billion)	$2.5-$3.0
Trade Deficit (Billion)	$2.0-$2.5
Exports (Billion)	$69.5
Imports (Billion)	$75-$76
Wholesale Prices (Annual Average)	8.0%-8.5%
Consumer Prices (Annual Average)	9.0%-9.5%

Source: Republic of Korea Embassy, Washington, DC (1990).

Table A-13: Growth in Consumption of Luxury Goods in Korea ($M)

Item	1989 ($ Millions)	January-September 1990 ($ Millions)	Percentage Growth
Home Appliances	95.0	126.0	32.6
TV Sets	13.0	19.5	50.0
Electric Appliances for Home	59.8	81.2	35.8
Sedans	23.2	55.2	137.9
Musical Instruments	20.2	25.2	24.8
Audio Equipment	81.3	84.7	4.2
Plastic Goods	56.9	84.3	48.2
Sundry Goods	365.5	565.4	54.7
Total	905.1	1,303.9	44.1

Source: Republic of Korea Embassy, Washington, DC (1991).

Table A-14: Price Comparisons of Selected Goods and Services

	Dinner	Beer	Alka Seltzer	Laundered Shirt
Beijing	22.29	8.53	7.56	1.72
Hong Kong	34.07	2.62	4.73	1.58
Singapore	28.00	9.47	5.88	2.01
Sydney	24.82	6.06	5.35	2.47
Tokyo	61.94	11.44	NA	3.18

Note: These are average prices in the countries shows in U.S. dollars and include sales tax and value added tax where appropriate.

Source: Runzheimer International, Reports on Travel Management (Monthly), Northbrook, IL 60062 (Tel: 414/534-3121).

Table A-15: Currency Equivalence and Conversion (January 1992)

Country	Currency	Equivalent	Equivalent to One U.S. Dollar
Hong Kong	1 Dollar	100 Cents	7.80
Indonesia	1 Rupiah	100 Son	1,663.00
Japan	1 Yen	100 Sen	120.00
Korea	1 Won	100 Chön	637.00
Malaysia	1 Ringgit (Dollar)	100 Sen	2.36
Philippines	1 Peso	100 Centavos	23.00
Singapore	1 Dollar	100 Cents	1.50
Taiwan	1 Dollar	100 Cents	24.00
Thailand	1 Baht	100 Satangs	22.63

Source: Thomas Cook Currency Services, Inc. (January 1992).

Table A-16: Largest National Economies
(Top 25 Compared with Washington, DC)

	GNP $ Billions
1. United States	4,881
2. Japan	2,856
3. Soviet Union	2,526
4. Germany	1,400
5. France	920
6. United Kingdom	802
7. Italy	797
8. People's Republic of China	546
9. Canada	472
10. Brazil	373
11. Spain	330
12. Iran	318
13. India	269
14. Australia	230
15. Netherlands	226
16. Switzerland	189
17. Poland	180
18. Sweden	175
19. South Korea	169
20. Belgium	149
21. Czechoslovakia	138
22. Austria	124
** Metropolitan Washington D.C.	120
23. Taiwan	119
24. Romania	118
25. Denmark	104

Source: Greater Washington Research Center.

**Table 17: Telephone Traffic with the United States
(Selected Countries from the Top 50 by Revenues)**

	US$ Billion
Mexico	533.9
West Germany	167.2
Philippines	114.8
South Korea	111.6
Japan	78.5
United Kingdom	46.2
Taiwan	45.0
Poland	36.2
France	32.9
Thailand	30.2
People's Republic of China	26.4
Indonesia	14.7
Hong Kong	14.1
Yugoslavia	12.5
Malaysia	12.1
Romania	8.4
Jordan	7.9

Note: Includes voice telephony, datacom, telex, and telegraph traffic.
Source: U.S. Federal Communications Commission, *Statistics of Communications Common Carriers*, September 1990.

Table A-18: Weighted Ranking of U.S. Trade Partners by Opportunity (Listed Alphabetically Within Each Group)

Group 1

Belgium	Hong Kong	Netherlands
Brazil	India	Saudi Arabia
Canada	Italy	Spain
China	Japan	Taiwan
France	Korea	United Kingdom
Germany		

Group 2

Australia	Pakistan	Thailand
Austria	Singapore	Turkey
Chile	South Africa	Venezuela
Colombia	Sweden	United Arab Emirates
Indonesia	Switzerland	U.S.S.R.
Malaysia		

Group 3

Algeria	Greece	Panama
Argentina	Ireland	Philippines
Czechoslovakia	Israel	Poland
Denmark	Nigeria	Portugal
Egypt	Norway	Yugoslavia
Finland		

Group 4

Barbados	Honduras	Morocco
Cameroon	Hungary	New Zealand
Costa Rica	Ivory Coast	Peru
Dominican Republic	Jamaica	Romania
Ecuador	Kenya	Trinidad and Tobago
Guatemala		

Note: Iraq and Kuwait are not ranked due to economic conditions at time of assessment in October 1991.

Weighting factors include: GNP/GDP; imports of manufactured goods and U.S. exports of manufacturers; political, social, geographic, and strategic conditions; projected annual dollar gain through 1992 in import market, U.S. exports, and total consumption; projected change in U.S. share of import market; competition for U.S. exporters from local domestic suppliers and third-country suppliers; barriers to market access for U.S. exporters; and industry market priority. (Ranked on 1-5 scale.)

Source: U.S. Department of Commerce. International Trade Administration. 1991.

Table A-19: Consumer Gasoline Prices
(Comparison with Selected Locations)

	U.S. Dollar
Abidjan, Ivory Coast	4.31
Milan, Italy	4.11
Moscow	3.85
Managua, Nicaragua	3.82
Stockholm	3.80
Tokyo	3.57
Helsinki	3.51
Paris	3.46
Dublin	3.45
Copenhagen	3.39
Oslo	3.30
Lisbon	3.25
Amsterdam	3.13
Atlanta, Georgia	0.97
Jakarta, Indonesia	0.90
Abu Dhabi, UAE	0.83
Manama, Bahrain	0.80
Mexico City	0.79
Santo Domingo, Dominican Republic	0.71
Cairo	0.70
Bogota, Colombia	0.69
Riyadh, Saudi Arabia	0.60
Kuwait	0.52
Quito, Ecuador	0.40
Lagos, Nigeria	0.21
Caracas, Venezuela	0.21

Source: Runzheimer International, *Reports on Travel Management* (Monthly), Northbrook, IL 60062 (Tel: 414/534-3121).

Table A-20: BERI Political Risk Index Rating (Lowest Risk Countries)

	1990	+1 Year (Projected)	+5 Years (Projected)
1. Switzerland	78	78	77
2. Singapore	75	75	75
3. Japan	70	73	72
4. Norway	70	70	72
5. Germany	68	67	70
6. Taiwan	68	68	70
7. United States	70	68	70
8. Australia	69	67	68
9. Netherlands	68	68	68
10. Sweden	68	67	68

Source: Business Environment Risk Information (BERI) Washington, DC (1990).

Table A-21: Average ROI for U.S. Foreign Investment (1984-1988)

Singapore	37.4
South Korea	28.5
Spain	25.8
Italy	25.6
Hong Kong	24.4
Japan	24.4
Nigeria	22.4
Taiwan	21.5
Portugal	21.1
Ireland	20.9
Netherlands	20.9
Belgium	20.1
Denmark	19.5
France	19.2
Austria	17.7
Thailand	17.8
United Kingdom	16.9
All Countries	16.8

Source: U.S. Department of Commerce (1990).

Table A-22: International Competitiveness Index of Ten Newly Industrialized Economies

	Singapore	Hong Kong	Taiwan	Korea	Malaysia	Thailand	Indonesia
Overall	1	2	3	4	5	6	9
Dynamism of the Economy	1	4	2	3	5	7	9
Industrial Efficiency	1	2	4	3	5	6	8
Dynamism of the Market	2	1	3	5	6	9	7
Financial Dynamism	1	2	3	4	5	6	9
Human Resources	1	3	2	4	5	6	9
State Interference	2	1	3	8	6	4	9
Natural Endowments	10	9	8	5	1	7	3
Outward Orientation	1	3	2	4	5	7	9
Innovative Forward Orientation	2	7	1	3	5	6	10
Sociopolitical Stability	1	2	4	7	3	5	6

1 = High   10 = Low

Note: India, Brazil and Mexico were also included in this survey.
Source: The World Competitiveness Report (1989) published by the International Management Development Institute and the World Economic Forum (Geneva Switzerland).

Index

Malaysia

ABOUT THE AUTHORS

OLIVER C. DZIGGEL

Oliver C. Dziggel is President of Enterprise Development International, Inc. (EDI), a high technology firm based in Washington, D.C. specializing in international business development and technology transfer in Eastern and Western Europe, Latin America, the Pacific Rim, and Africa. Prior to founding EDI, Mr. Dziggel managed MCI's antitrust litigations in the precedent-setting actions which resulted in the total restructuring of the U.S. telecom industry. He also achieved significant accomplishments with ITT WorldCom, International Data Corporation, and Booz-Allen & Hamilton. Mr. Dziggel earned his Masters degree in International Affairs from The George Washington University in Washington, D.C., and a Masters-equivalent in European integration from the Friedrich-Wilhelm Universität in Bonn, Germany.

ALLYN ENDERLYN

Allyn Enderlyn is Senior Vice President and co-founder of Enterprise Development International, Inc. (EDI). She is Project Manager for the Telecommunications and Electronics Consortium in Eastern Europe (one of the five Consortia of American Businesses in Eastern Europe — CABEE — a component of the American Business and Private Sector Development Initiative, a joint effort of the Commerce Department and the Agency for International Development). The Telecommunications Industry Association is the recipient of that grant.

Ms. Enderlyn is the Executive Vice President of the National Association of Women Business Owners (NAWBO). She has also held leadership positions for the past fifteen years in other organizations. Ms. Enderlyn has co-authored numerous trade volumes for other regions of the world. She and Mr. Dziggel are currently writing a book on *Cracking Latin America*. She has a B.A. from The American University and an M.B.A. in Finance and Investments from The George Washington University.